Break Through
Featuring
Tiffany Brickhouse

Break Through Featuring Tiffany Brickhouse

Powerful Stories
from Global Authorities
That Are Guaranteed
to Equip Anyone for
Real Life Breakthrough

Tiffany Brickhouse

Johnny Wimbrey

Nik Halik

Les Brown

and other leading authorities

WIMBREY TRAINING SYSTEMS
SOUTHLAKE, TEXAS

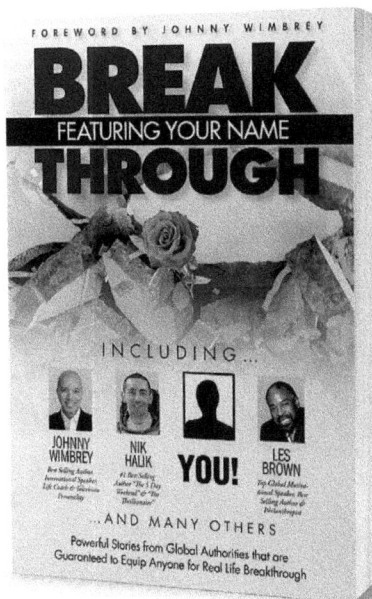

TABLE OF CONTENTS

Foreword

Think back to the hardest, darkest times in your life. What were you going through? How many times did you fail? How did you break through the difficulties and barriers you faced? How did you finally reach the success you knew you deserved?

Why do I ask this? Why do I care about the bad times and failures in your life? I care because how you handled the bad times tell me what type of person you are. I care because the choices you make when you face failure and the lessons you learn as you break through define you.

I can feel your skepticism. You think, really? Failure's important? Why?

Well, I know this to be true. I have had failures and troubles, and my choices turned me into the man I am today. I managed to break past and break through those times.

This is true, too, with the amazing group of authors I have asked to join me in *Break Through*.

I am honored to be joined by the men and women who have made deliberate sacrifices to contribute chapters to this book. Les Brown, Nik Halik, and every one of our other authors will inspire you with their stories of how they broke through their failures and barriers.

All had pain, rejection, and setbacks, and all were able to assess where they were and to make the necessary choices. Every author honestly shares their mistakes and successes with us.

Our *Break Through* authors are brave and fascinating, full of faith in their futures, and generous with their truths. They will help you navigate the crossroads you encounter and help you make sure your choices send you down the path of empowerment, confidence, and success. I am confident they will help you on your journey.

I introduce you now to my *Break Through* partners. Each one is someone I am proud to call a co-author and friend.

—Johnny Wimbrey

CHAPTER ONE

Inspect What You Expect

Johnny Wimbrey

There are many things upon which I am not an authority, and there are many areas in which I will never be able to claim to be an expert, but I can tell you with total confidence that I *am* the authority on the expectation of success.

Every day, I wake up with the expectation for another level of success. I *expect* to find success mentally, emotionally, spiritually, financially, with love, with compassion, and with sensitivity.

I know I will have more of everything that matters to me, and it's just not material things. I crave and expect more knowledge, more honesty, and more good people in my life. My expectation is not arrogant, it's not greedy. My expectation is an intrinsic part of me, and I have honed it and practiced it since I was eighteen years old.

I am Johnny Wimbrey. I am a public speaker and entrepreneur, known around the world for inspiring people and helping them to change their lives. I have built a wonderful life with my wife and children. Now I'm in the privileged position of being able to give back to my community and around the globe. No one, myself included, would have expected this—let alone predicted it—based on who I used to be. The choices I made, however, made me the man I am today.

Rejection framed my young life. My earliest memory is being hungry in a shelter for battered women. I was three years old and wanted some milk that I found when I opened the refrigerator door. Someone slammed the door on my fingers and told me the refrigerator wasn't ours and the milk wasn't mine to drink because it belonged to another family at the shelter.

That was probably the moment I grasped the unhappy facts: Yes, my mother had left my abusive, alcoholic father; we were temporary guests in a battered women's shelter; my two older brothers and I were homeless.

That feeling of rejection became the mainstay of my childhood and adolescence. My brothers, mother, and I had fled from Texas to California and I didn't see my father for years. I thought he rejected us.

My mother sent us back to live with him a few years later, and I didn't see her for the next three years of my life. More rejection. It was better to think she was dead than she had rejected us. I spent my elementary school years with my unpredictable, alcoholic father who was always busy, doing my best to keep up with my two big brothers: one a future felon, the other a future minister.

I didn't ask to move to California; I didn't ask to be sent back away from my mother, I definitely didn't ask to live with my father again. Looking back, though, I'm so glad I did live with him during those formative years. He gave me the basis for my understanding of expectation.

My father worked as a trash collector for the city. He didn't work in our poor neighborhood; his route took him over to the other side of town, the *rich* side of town. Every year when we had the long Christmas school holiday, my dad took us three boys along after work.

My father wanted us to see what else was out there in the world. He wanted us to see all the things we could have. He pushed us to open our eyes to the innumerable possibilities we had in front of us. Those trips taught me to despise the word *average*. My father raised my expectations. Not then, but later in my adolescence, I took it upon myself to rise to the challenge.

My own expectation for daily increase comes from a garbage man who refused to allow me to accept "average." He taught me to train my vision.

It took me a while to perfect this vision. It was focused on the wrong things in high school, when I made some of the worse decisions of my life. Unfortunately, my focus involved cigarettes, alcohol, drugs, and guns. My teachers told me they saw potential and talent in me and I ignored them. Who were they to tell me how to run my life? I was barreling down a one-way path headed to gang violence, substance abuse, prison, and a literal dead end.

When I was eighteen years old and a junior in high school, my path took a sudden turn when my good friend Mookie was killed by a rival. I went to Mookie's wake to say goodbye, and my brain was teeming with thoughts of death, grief, anger, and vengeance. I packed my gun as I got dressed that evening. I was looking for revenge, ready for a fight, with no glimmer of consequences or the future in my thoughts.

Brooding in my pew, I was barely listening to the speakers until Mookie's mother got up. I knew her, so I gave her the courtesy of listening to her fully. She talked with grace about my dear friend, her son, expressing not only her pain for his loss but actual forgiveness. She stood in front of Mookie's friends, family, and community and forgave her son's murderer. There was no room for interpretation:

"I forgive the man who shot my son."

She could have easily given in to her own anger and thoughts of revenge. She could have lashed out at those who loved her or withdrawn from her life altogether. But she didn't. If Mookie's *own mother*, the woman who loved him more than anyone else on this earth did, could forgive, what right did *I* have to seek vengeance?

A switch went on in my brain. I *knew* this moment was going to change my life. I knew my sudden awareness came straight from God. I was sitting there, conscious and aware, and I heard it clearly, just as if He had leaned over and whispered it directly into my ear: *This will change your life.*

I didn't hear Him because I was better or smarter than everyone around me; I was just ready to listen. God's message was flowing over everyone who was sitting with me; I was tuned to "receive."

I leaned forward and looked up and down the pew. My friends were radiating energy and anger. I could almost see the waves of vengeance coming off their bodies. Two seconds earlier, I was just like them. No more. The moment I changed, sitting there in the pew at Mookie's wake, I knew I expected more than I had the moment before.

My body stilled and I started breathing deeply. If I could have seen into the future, I would have known that every one of Mookie's and my friends would get long-term prison sentences. Perhaps I already did know this.

I knew we had been headed down the same path to the same dead end. I knew I could have more than this. *I could be more than this.*

After everyone said their "peace" and we were milling around outside, I pulled Reverend Fitzgerald aside.

"Can I talk to you for a second?"

"Of course, son. What is it?"

"I want to give you my gun. If I give you my gun, I know I won't do anything crazy. Reverend, please take it. I don't want to live like this anymore. I am serious this time."

"You know if you give this to me, I'm not going to give it back."

"Yes, sir."

That was it. I gave him my gun. I stopped selling drugs. I stopped breaking the law. I just stopped. The next day I met Crystal, who became my wife a few years later.

I walked away from the life I had been leading. I said I was changing. And I did.

I was blessed with the chance to take what I had been given and use it to climb up and out. My prayers, my conversations with God, and the knowledge that He would give me what I needed when I needed it most, helped me every step of the way. My accomplishments didn't just belong to me; I knew I was being watched and constantly assisted. Instead of giving me complacency, my knowledge that I was never completely alone gave me both comfort and the confidence I needed to take matters into my own hands.

I began to inspect, what I expect.

It saddens me that people feel guilty for expecting more. Why is this the case? Why do they feel uncomfortable if they *expect* more success? Why do they dial back on that verb and replace it with a less aggressive one like "hope?"

The meaning completely changes when you *hope* for more success, or *hope* for better health, or *hope* to improve your financial situation. You give up all involvement and responsibility. You just give up.

There are times when hope has a place in your life and your spiritual and mental process. One never wants to lose hope for your child's continued happiness in life or hope for world peace.

There is a place for hope.

When it comes to your success and things over which you can or could have input and control, you need to **expect**.

My expectations are the basis of my success. Despite the hardships in my life, I can honestly tell you with unwavering confidence I have *never* just been satisfied with what I have so far.

I wake up every day expecting success.

I wish this were an audio book so you could hear the passion in my voice in the words that you are reading right now: I have never entertained a lifestyle of decrease; I have never thought to myself, "this is it." You absolutely, without question deserve your achievements and there is nothing wrong with waking up every day expecting exactly that!

Sashin Govender is a prime example of someone who internalized the concept of expectation at a young age. He accompanied his father to my seminars before he was a teenager, and he was not a shy, self-conscious 12-year old. Sashin sat up front and gave me every ounce of his attention.

He put my teachings to work as soon as he was able and hit his first million by the time he was 20. Now, at 23, he is a multimillionaire and speaks on stages around the world.

As he was getting started, he called me almost every day. He never had a little voice in the back of his head that told him that he was bothering me, that it was too many phone calls, that he needed to dial it back. I recognized his hunger and mindset and I gave him direct access whenever he wanted.

Sashin was very young when he heard the concept *expectation to increase*. He was not jaded or tired; he hadn't grown up with limitations on his future. He knew that if he focused on limitation, that's what he would get.

He works like he is broke, every day, and he never stops to count his successes or rest on his laurels. Because he internalizes his expectation to increase, he's growing exponentially, and he'll have his first million-dollar year within two years.

There is so much power in *expectation*. Getting you to the mindset of expecting results will catapult you into a life that most people only dream of having. I want you to get to the mindset and determination of success in the exact same way that when you take a breath you *expect* oxygen, the exact same way that you *expect* a chair to hold you up when you sit down, the exact same way you *expect* the electricity to work when you turn on the lights.

You need to have that exact same expectation for personal triumph. Every day of your life you should wake up with an expectation of success.

It can start for you now. Inspect what you expect! Everyday, *expect* increase and I promise you, *your personal Break Through is imminent!*

Biography

Johnny Wimbrey is a speaker, author, trainer, and motivator, working with sales teams, high-profile athletes, politicians, and personalities around the world.

He has launched three companies—Wimbrey Training Systems, Wimbrey Global, and Royal Success Club International—and heads a sales team of thousands in more than 50 countries, overseeing an active customer database of half a million families.

Johnny shares his powerful message through speaking engagements around the world. He also has a wide media following and has appeared as a guest expert and panelist on television shows including the *Steve Harvey Show, E! News,* and *The Today Show.*

Johnny's first book, *From the Hood to Doing Good,* has sold more than 200,000 copies in printed and digital editions.

Johnny has collaborated on several other books including *Conversations of Success* and *Multiple Streams of Determination;* combined, they have more than 500,000 copies in print.

Johnny regularly speaks for non-profit organizations and reunites children with their families from whom they've been separated for years due to government action. He and his wife, Crystal, are co-founders of Wimbrey WorldWide Ministries, a non-profit which has built six schools in Central America and helped fund water purification systems in Africa.

Contact Information:

Johnny D. Wimbrey
Master Motivation/Success Trainer

Most Requested Topics:
Motivation/Keynote
Overcoming Adversity
Youth Enrichment
Leadership/Sales

www.johnnywimbrey.com

 @Wimbrey

 @Wimbrey

 @Wimbrey

 JohnnyWimbrey

 @Wimbrey

 LinkedIn@Wimbrey

CHAPTER TWO

Target the Excellence That Lives Inside You

John Ramsey

The day my life began to change, my wife and I were homeless and down to our last dollar. I am not just using that term to make a point. I mean, literally, we had *one dollar* to our name.

This was just over 20 years ago, and my life had taken a sudden downturn, as is happening now to so many. We had lost our home and I didn't know how I was going to provide for my family. I had often heard *when the student is ready, the teacher will appear,* yet I was surprised when a man showed up on my path. That day I learned the lesson that started me on my path to excellence.

"Do you know how to pray, John?" he asked.

I looked up with tears in my eyes, and said, "I guess so."

I quickly learned I was wrong—I was begging, not praying. When I began to honestly pray and focus on the principles he taught me, my life changed.

That day I learned prayer isn't meant to impress others. Your words have absolutely nothing to do with what you receive from the kingdom of God. So, stop begging God. He already knows what you need. He's waiting for you.

Do you want to see a change in your life? Do you have obstacles to overcome? You must learn how to pray! All of us need to hear God. The Kingdom of God is real, and it all starts with prayer. Embrace His spirit *today!*

God wants to help you because He knows you can do anything with His help. Proverbs 3:5 tells us *Trust in the Lord with all your heart and lean not on your own understanding* (New International Version). That's not always easy to do, and it means you acknowledge that you don't have the answers and you're going to have to trust Him to lead you.

In 1999, my ego was much bigger than my bank account. I quickly discovered I couldn't use His plan for my life if I didn't listen to what He has to say. Prayer is more than just talking to God—it involves a *lot* of listening.

Is anyone of you in trouble? He should pray. (James 5:13, NIV)

Notice the bible doesn't say "Let him call his best friend," or "Let him Google what to do." It says PRAY. When people are in trouble, they need to pray. And don't tell me you can't hear God. You *can* hear God, you really can—you just don't recognize His voice. God's voice sounds like your own thoughts. You just have to recognize when He's talking.

I had to hear God. I *had* to. In prayer, God began to lead me out of my mess.

He'll lead you to victory too, if you will go before Him with a sincere heart, pray, and ask Him to show you what to do.

೨ ೨ ೨

As I pen these words, it's 2020. My life has changed in so many ways! I now expect excellence from the moment I awake, and I rely on my favorite book, "the book of good news."

Consider it pure joy, my brothers, whenever you face trials of many kinds because you know that the testing of your faith develops perseverance. Perseverance must finish its work so that you may be mature and complete, not lacking anything. (James 1:2-4, NIV)

Twenty years ago, I found it hard to "consider it pure joy" when I faced trials of any kind. What I felt was not pure joy, but misery. While I knew God had not abandoned me, I still felt miserable. James reminds us that the trials we face are for *growing* our faith. It is precisely *because* we place our faith in God that we face trials. These trials, whatever they may mean to another person, are there to increase our commitment to God.

Now here is the point you must understand: I was not as strong in the Word then as I am now. When we go through trials, one misery is our inability to discern either the purpose or the duration of the trial. Understanding our human weaknesses, James instructs us to ask God for wisdom, and not just any wisdom. We are to ask for the wisdom to weather our trials and to look to the goodness of God, even when we're unable to look beyond the trials of the moment.

Whatever you desire is waiting for you to claim it. All you must do is focus on what you want. You must learn to trust yourself and the Power within you and know it will all work out. Your greatest obstacle to happiness is when you don't live in the present moment and don't follow your joy. The solution is simple: Do just the opposite. When you find yourself focusing on the past or the future, remind yourself that the present

13

moment is all there is, and surrender to what is happening *now.* You'll see how life suddenly starts working for you.

If you put the same amount of effort into finding what gives you joy as you put into working at a job you dislike, you'll end up with results that will make you wonder, "Why did I wait so long to do this?"

ఌ ఌ ఌ

Your life's purpose

When you have a purpose in life, you enjoy your life every day. More importantly, you give your conscious mind, your subconscious mind, and your spirit a reason for existing—you give them a mission and a direction. This reason and direction lead you to even more opportunities that fulfill your purpose and help you enjoy life even more.

Here's how it works. Your purpose in life is driven by an underlying feeling or emotion. Your subconscious mind picks up on the emotion and the purpose and begins attracting more good situations, positive people, and beneficial events to help you fulfill that purpose and enjoy life.

If you feel that you're going through the day without any real purpose and you want to have a purpose, you're halfway there. There is a purpose to each day, but you're just not recognizing it. For instance, let's say you work as a grocery store cashier and you go to work each day thinking that your job has no purpose, your life has no purpose, and you're just going through the motions.

Try a different way of looking at it: Your job as a grocery store cashier is a valuable, brave service, especially in a time of pandemic or crisis. Even in good times, your job helps make the shoppers' experience more pleasant and efficient, helps your bosses keep track of inventory and profits, and helps the company make sure that people pay for what they buy in a quick and easy manner. Do you see how what you thought was a mundane job really has a lot of purposes if you look at things a little differently?

You may say: "All right, I see it for the job, but I don't feel like I'm *living* with any real purpose." There is a lot that we can do to help you live with purpose.

First, look at how you spend your day. Grab a notepad and pen and describe in detail exactly how you spend your time, then look at the schedule closely and see how many hours have been set aside for *you*—when you get to have some time to yourself when you can do whatever you want without anyone bothering you.

If you find you have little or no time for yourself, then you've recognized the first step to finding your purpose.

Too often when people feel they don't have any purpose, I have found they've never set aside time just for themselves. Don't misunderstand, I don't mean your purpose is to do whatever you want, whenever you want. But having some time set aside for yourself allows you to discover your purpose. When your schedule is so packed you have no time for yourself, you can't look inside yourself and discover your purpose.

Please set some time aside just for you. I know you're thinking, "John, I come home at the end of a long day; I have three kids to feed and a spouse to care for. By the time I'm done, I barely have energy or time for anything else." Fair enough. I'm not asking you to take an hour-long bubble bath or go for a 10-mile run. Take just five minutes for yourself. Read something fun and light, have a glass of wine, go for a short walk, stretch out on your bed, and relax—anything you enjoy for five dedicated minutes. After a week, stretch the time to ten minutes. It's *your* time, so just do something you want to do.

When you calm down and are more at peace, when your mind and body are at rest, your subconscious mind goes to work because it is no longer being bombarded with all kinds of distracting stimulus and information. Instead, your subconscious will help you find ways to enjoy your life and find your purpose.

At this point, try looking at your life a little differently. I call this process "changing your glasses," and it'll give you the right pair to see clearly.

In the case of the person who's had a long day, three kids to feed, and a spouse to care for, well, this person already has a tremendous purpose. It may not be the ideal dream life, but there is a purpose. And here's how it gets better: When you recognize the purpose, you attract more positive things into your life. Why? Because when you finally recognize your purpose, you see things in a more positive way. This releases a tremendous amount of positive energy and positive vibrations and emotions which are picked up by your subconscious mind, and in turn, this attracts more positive situations.

Some of you will still say, "John, I do all that, but I still don't feel I have any purpose in my life." If this is the case, then you must start doing what you enjoy. Yes, you may have kids to feed or someone to care for, and yes, that may be the purpose for now—but if you still feel empty, then you *must* take some time to do what you enjoy. This activity won't necessarily be your purpose, but by doing what you enjoy even for a few minutes a day, you'll eventually discover your purpose.

You'll have started a process, and part of that process requires that you enjoy life, relax, and understand that whatever you focus on, you will attract.

Don't be Worried about Making a Mistake

This is the time in the growth process that many people lose momentum or freeze their growth, afraid of heading in the wrong direction or making mistakes. Don't be afraid, for it's certain that you will make many mistakes in this process. You've been programmed since childhood to look at your mistakes, examine them, pick them to death, and worry about them.

We've been brought up with a belief system that says we should constantly judge ourselves, evaluate ourselves, and see if we are doing it "right." You've been taught to concentrate on what isn't, what should be, and what could have been. We end up judging ourselves so harshly that we quit producing results because we are afraid to make mistakes.

It's okay to make mistakes. You might as well face this fact; there is no security between the cradle and the grave. The only security that you and I have is our ability to create and produce results. If we are not tied to the belief that we should not make mistakes, uncertainty won't be a problem. I've made a lot of mistakes in my life. Some of them were very large, but that is part of the growth process.

Utilizing the Power of Purpose

To get the most out of your Power of Purpose, you need to think about your purpose regularly. I don't mean contemplating it once a week or once a month; you must think about all the positive things you do every day that have a purpose, impacting your life and the lives of those around you.

If you're a cashier working in a supermarket, think about the good deeds you do every day for your customers and fellow employees and how your actions benefit them. If you're a parent, think about all the positive, supportive actions that you do for your children as you help them learn and grow up. If you're an elderly person on social security, think about the kind and affirmative act that you do during the day, and remember all of the positive things that you have done in your life.

Every positive thing that you do has a purpose—it has an impact on you and the people around you.

When you focus on your positive purpose, you simply attract more positive things into your life. You won't see changes overnight, although I know most of you would like to see instant changes. You have to give your mind and subconscious mind time to work and attract the situations you need to help you improve your life. If you do this just for a few weeks or months, you'll end up right back where you were. You must continue focusing on your positive actions until it becomes a *habit*. Practice this habit every day for the rest of your life without even thinking about it.

Some of you will say, "Every day for the rest of my life? I don't have time for that!" Fine, then your next option is to stay where you are for the rest of your life—and if where you are is good enough, great! Enjoy it. If it isn't, then you owe it to yourself to make the improvements and changes that will allow you to truly enjoy life. The Power of Purpose will do that for you.

Without the Power of Purpose, your chances for succeeding are slim to none.

'Without a VISION, the people perish.'

A vision is defined as a mental image produced by the imagination.

For years I struggled with maintaining a vision, and I had no clear and consistent vision of where I truly wanted to go. I was always busy, and when I had a vision, I'd be distracted and forget about it within a couple of weeks. Has this ever happened to you?

Open a biography of every successful athlete, entertainer, or entrepreneur, and you'll discover they each had a vision of the path they were pursuing. Your vision doesn't have to be an instantly clear-cut masterpiece—it needs to evolve. What's important is to start building a clear mental image of your future.

Here are three vital questions to ask yourself:

What do you want people to say about you 100 years from now?

How do you want to leave the world a better place?

What is the *vision* for your life, for your business, family, relationships?

Hold that vision. Keep it in your mind. Read it out loud when you first get up in the morning. Right before you go to bed, affirm it. Embrace it. Ponder it. Expand it.

Perhaps you had a vision years ago; it's time to bring it back to your life today. Start thinking about your vision. You'll start to feel energized. You'll start to regain that winning spirit. You've heard *Start with the end in mind.* Now it's time to do it.

Have the courage to speak this out loud, and with energy:

I am a person of vision, power, and excellence!

My brightest days are ahead of me!

Nothing and no one can stop you from creating the life you desire. The only one who can stop you is yourself and your own limiting beliefs. I discovered by challenging the conviction of what you believe about yourself, you begin the transformation process. Life is to be lived by design, not default. Make a decision right now that you are open, responsive, and receptive to new ideas and beliefs that will support you in creating the life you desire.

When faith enters your life, fortune isn't far behind.

Biography

John Ramsey is an internationally recognized entrepreneur and business consultant, specializing in leadership development, prosperity consciousness, and mindset training. As president of Targeting Excellence, he's committed to empowering people by helping them change the way they see and feel about themselves in order to create the life they desire.

John has been married to the love of his life, Antoinette, since 2016, and they live in Dallas, Texas. Collectively, they have six children and 10 grandchildren.

Contact Information

Website: TargetingExcellence.com
Email: TargetingExcellence777@gmail.com

CHAPTER THREE

Finding My Voice

Toni Fowlkes

R umor has it we attract our own fate. The terrible thing about rumors, though, is they are often just lies. Do young children deserve to attract the attention of pedophiles? Is it the robbery victim's fault that a gun-toting criminal wreaks havoc upon them?

The answer is *no*.

These lies pin every one of those unfortunate events on victims, leaving us with feelings of guilt and unworthiness that sometimes never go away.

Not everything is fair. It's about what God allows, what He doesn't, and what we do in response. It's about us seeing He is present in everything. It's about the stories that lead us back to Him.

Truth be told . . .

Should I be completely honest? How honest is too honest? The truth is, writing this is the hardest thing that I have ever done, and at the same time telling my truth is the best thing I have ever done for myself. I want to help someone else's breakthrough, and I pray that your eyes will be as freed reading my words as I am writing them. Though my life has had its share of pain and trouble, I don't identify as a victim. That's not who I am.

Who am I? There's so much to me it's hard to begin, but at the core, I am just a woman who loves God and wants Him to use every bit of my story for His glory. Not all of my life was painful, but I promised you the brutal truth and I am going to give it to you.

From the very beginning, I was unsure of who I was. I knew my name, but for the longest time, I didn't know if I belonged to the family I lived with. No, I'm serious. My mom and sisters joked that they'd found me in the trash can.

People always asked if I belonged because my last name wasn't the same as my siblings' and as a fair-skinned little girl with red hair and a speech impediment, I was different from everyone else in our proud black Louisiana family. I had no father. I don't know who he is, and I'm okay with it now. But then, it was confusing.

I may not have come out of trash can, but I believed that somehow my family thought I was trash. After all, only trash belongs in the trash can.

Why did God even make me? I asked myself that every day. I didn't bother asking God because I blamed Him for everything sometimes. I hated my life."

"Girl, who are you and why should I care?" you ask.

It's all right. I'm not offended by that question. I am a single mother of an amazing teenage daughter. I am an author, speaker, singer, ministry consultant, civil mediator, and I lead worship on Sundays, effecting change everywhere I go. I've always known my story would be heard. I had no idea, though, how long my journey would be.

As a child, I did have many good times, too. My mom had me focus on music rather than sports because she thought it would afford me the most opportunities. She was right about that. Music was my escape. I excelled, making my way into national honors bands and even playing at the Clinton Inaugural Festival. I made decent grades, was an artist, sang in chorus, and was active in clubs. I adored my mom, we had fun as a family, and my childhood was sprinkled with trips to Disney and the beaches. I am grateful for everything I had.

God Allowed It

When I was about ten, my mom was earning her college degree while working as a juvenile probation officer, so my brother and I were alone a lot. Mom was good friends with a fellow student, a teacher working on his graduate degree. My mom was always busy, and he knew it. I was a fatherless child yearning for a father, and he knew it.

The first time he came to "check" on my brother and me, he stayed just a few minutes. My baby brother was upstairs playing with his Tonka trucks, and I was downstairs getting "hugged." His hugs were long, and sort of sweaty. They were tight, and he shook a lot. Sometimes, especially when I got older, I noticed that he looked like he had an accident on himself. Sometimes he would try to kiss me. To this day, I hate the smell of the gum he chewed.

I was ten. What did I know?

For a long time, though I hated those hugs, I let his visits be a part of our routine. I felt like I had a grown friend who understood me. He cared about me. He *saw* me, and that was important. In the world outside of home, I never fit in anywhere. I needed his friendship, but I didn't want his hugs.

I remember how I felt after his visits. I felt dirty. I felt gross. I'd take long, really hot baths, and sometimes I would rub my entire body with cotton balls and alcohol to bathe away the filth I felt inside me. As I grew older, the visits happened less and less, but I always answered his calls and never said a word to anyone about the visits.

What You Can't See
Will Hurt You

Being molested or sexually assaulted messes you up, so sometimes even with the best therapy (which I had), you never completely understand the *why*, the *how*, or *why am I like this?* It changes how you see things, always. It disrupts the trajectory of your life in such a profound way, you don't know who you'd have been if it had never happened.

Years later, I was in a relationship that seemed perfect from the outside. We definitely had some serious issues, but back then all I knew is that I wanted to be married and accepted. My fiancé was much older, and from my experience as a child, I felt more wanted when I was with an older man. Sick, right? We had the houses, the cars, and looked great at galas and church. I had the life so many of my peers wanted, but I was dying inside.

I was dying because I was bulimarexic. You read it right. Bulimia is purging after eating and anorexia is not eating much, if at all. I began as anorexic my senior year with diet pills, but by twenty I was not eating (and purging if I did) and taking stronger diet pills and laxatives.

I was skinny already, 5'9", 120 pounds. So, why, you ask? When your mind is made up that you ain't worth anything and people only want you for your "hugs," you try every avenue available to fix what is wrong with you. According to my doctor, my eating disorder was caused by my need to control something in my life. He also told me that eventually, my organs would begin to suffer and shut down.

There were times when I thought the best thing would be to say goodbye to it all—take a ton of pills and die—but I didn't follow through.

I was a phony. Not in the sense that I wasn't kind, and loving, and funny, but in the sense that I hid my problems so no one could see. I believed with all my heart that if people knew how gross I was, they wouldn't want me around. So, I made sure no one ever knew the real me.

Being the person everyone loves isn't all bad, even when who they think you are is not all true. I was friendly and popular. I won beauty pageants. I had a great job. I had it all. To top it all off, I met God and began the never-ending journey of finding my true identity.

Yep. I met God.

I'd grown up in the Baptist church and was involved in *everything*. My mom is a powerful leader and effects change everywhere she went. People love her. My mom is everything I wanted to be, so church became home for me. I was the youth president and loved every minute of it, doing it because I needed to be accepted. Eventually, I began leading worship, and in that, I found my calling.

From the time when I was a little girl, I knew God wanted me to use my voice. The problem was I didn't think I had one. I had been a quiet child with a speech impediment. Once I began leading worship regularly, I felt closer to God. I was using my gifts and talents to serve God, and minister to people who were just like me, people who were hurting under the surface.

The ministry is who I am. However, I found myself ignoring the ugly truths about myself and obsessing over serving in church. It was a natural thing, but it wasn't always spiritual. That was the issue. Ministry should be spiritual. My heart was, and always will be for God, but my actions, many times, were to prove something to myself, not to God. I thought I had to please in order for Him to like me.

I Am Always With You

It was our annual Women's Day at church, a beautiful service, and I ministered both in song and sign language. I was exhausted, went home, the house was empty, and I found myself in my walk-in closet.

I don't know how I ended up with a bunch of my fiancé's ties around my neck, but I did. I was drained. Ministering isn't like motivational speaking. It's spiritual. I had given so much of myself and my spirit, and there I was in the closet, sitting on a shelf, about to end it all. I hated myself. I didn't hate myself for the thought of suicide, but because I had always hated me. I never liked me. I was sick of living, drained, and honestly just over it all. I believed I was worthless and I wanted things to be finished.

As I tightened the makeshift noose and just as I was contemplating jumping off the shelf, I felt heat in my face. It was very warm, intimidating, and I realized Satan was there, right in front of me, looking in my face—Satan, everyone's enemy. I could hear him laughing at me, daring me to jump.

Something happened. One of those unexplainable things that you see in movies. Just as sure as I knew Satan was in that closet laughing in my face, I felt the presence of God. He was there. When God is present you know it because you have "thoughts" that are not your own, just as when the enemy is present.

God said, "If he [Satan] is here, then I am here. He cannot be near you if I am not. And I am always with you."

Now, that sounds like a piece of scripture I've read before, but it was not my subconscious I was hearing. It was God, and He was in that closet with me. I knew at that moment that I didn't have to be afraid, that I had nothing to prove to anyone but God. He didn't just appear all of a sudden. God had always been there, though my focus hadn't been on Him. I'd been so focused on what I lacked that I felt only the enemy. I had allowed the enemy to tell me who I wasn't, rather than remembering who God told me I was.

Immediately after I heard God's voice, there was a knock on my closet door. That small knock was my daughter, but also God's way of saying, "Toni, I've been knocking on your heart." God had been saying to me all along that He wanted to come into my heart to show me true love, to show me how valuable I was to Him and His Kingdom.

I told my baby that I'd be out in a minute, then fell to my knees and begged God to hold my hand and keep me from ever doing that again.

It's gut-wrenching to think I would have left my daughter behind without a mother. It's hard to believe that a person could be so selfish, or self-consumed, or wrapped up in anguish that their own child's future is irrelevant for a moment. But remember, everything is spiritual.

When we hear of suicide, we think, *Wow. How could they do such a thing? How selfish. What were they thinking?* But for every problem, God has a solution that will show His glory in your life. He wants you to stick around to witness a miracle. Make no mistake, I know that it can feel impossible to see the light when everything around you is dark, and you're stumbling around, grabbing for something to hold on to. You have to keep walking forward, though. Eventually, you'll realize that as long as you're walking, you're a little bit closer to your destination.

You have to do it because there is a reason for your existence, and your reason is beautiful. Suicide is a result of being overcome by the fear of living in the future the way you have in the past. No one *has* to live in that fear, but ONLY God can defeat it.

Losing and finding my voice again.

One of the worst and most challenging times in my life was when I lost my voice. Not only did I grow up feeling I didn't have a voice, but when I began leading worship, I had a struggle with my physical vocal cords. I was new at leading full-time at a church, singing on a praise team at another church, and then

I started having issues with my voice. I am a classically trained vocalist, a coloratura soprano with lots of range yet undersized vocal cords (which I didn't know at the time). Suddenly, as I was singing, my voice would break from one octave to another with no warning. It wasn't subtle either; I could croak or sound like a dog whistle.

I lost all confidence in myself and my voice. My speaking voice was so raspy I earned the nickname Nanny Fran, after Fran Drescher. It changed everything and was traumatizing for me, as a leader. I saw a series of doctors, then specialists, and eventually found I had an autoimmune response to overusing my versatile but unfortunately small vocal cords. My body was attacking itself while I felt as though I was being attacked on every side of my life. I would cry for days at a time. I had to sit on the sidelines in church, watching others do what I felt I was called to do. This made me question my calling in its entirety. Did God call me to lead worship?

I had a lot of questions, but no voice to ask them with, and no answers. I rested my vocal cords for nearly a year. Once I retired from education, singing became much easier for me. I still have to take it easy on my voice, but I can sing again.

I learned that just because God calls you to do something doesn't mean you'll do it forever, or without a break. It made me a more patient teacher and brought out the true worshipper in me. There's nothing like singing your heart out to God with no voice, trusting He hears you anyway. And He does. He hears your heart. All He even *wants* is your heart.

Now, as a worship leader and ministry consultant, I have patience and don't judge the way I was judged. After all, the worship belongs to Him, not us. I realized my calling is not a job or position, but I am called to worship, as we all are.

Just Cause

Through my professional life as a civil mediator, I am familiar with the phrase "just cause," which is often used as a reason for firing someone. In my current career as a ministry consultant, I know churches use "just cause" to mean the sovereignty of God. I also use "just 'cause" to express my gratitude and humility for God's plan for me.

I will say with gratitude, just 'cause I thought I was ugly, just 'cause I was used, just 'cause I was bitter and suicidal, and even voiceless, it doesn't mean I was worthless. It means God allowed me to go through hard, ugly times so He could prove to me nothing could ever be so wrong that He wouldn't be present. God proved to me His love stands the tests of life and time.

He is proving it to you as well. You'll see God if you focus on Him and ignore the petty, ugly distractions of life.

You are reading this now just 'cause God has a perfect plan for you. Nothing you can ever do will drive God away from your path. He will find you. God won't rest until you come back to Him and know that everything you have gone through and will go through in the future is so someone else will hear your story and see Him. To Him, you are not just worthy, you are priceless.

Every day I decide to go on, doing my best, even though I don't have all of the answers. That is what life is—doing our best and leaving the unanswered questions to God.

Don't give up. If that means just getting out of bed some days, then *just get out of bed!*

My story isn't over, and your story isn't over either. No matter what, know that the next day comes and that it will get better if you focus on who you *are* and not who you *aren't.*

The day will come when your story will be heard, too.

Use your voice. *Tell your truth.*

Biography

Born in the Cajun town of Lake Charles, Louisiana, Toni Fowlkes attended McNeese State University, Louisiana State University, and is taking classes at Harvard University. She's on a slow track for a law degree.

Toni has many roles in her adult life, including as a speaker, civil mediator, an advocate for social justice, and a ministry consultant, which is her current focus.

Single and based in New Orleans, La., she homeschools her daughter, and the two of them travel widely.

Contact Information:

Email: ItsToniTime@gmail.com
Facebook: Toni Fowlkes
Instagram: ItsToniTime

CHAPTER FOUR

The TIKI Factor

Tiki Davis

A screwdriver in my neck at the age of nine nearly ended my life.

As it turned out, that blade would cut away my old existence and slice a path for a new beginning.

A man entered my bedroom and woke me. He asked harshly, *"Where is your mama, kid? Where is your mama, you little bastard? She stole my money!"*

I was not very afraid. I was accustomed to seeing men coming and going all the time in our home, so I sat up on the edge of the bed. "I don't know. Guess she's in the flats." The flats were the housing projects of Odessa, Texas.

But I never saw *this* coming.

The man wrapped a bandana around my neck and tried to strangle me. Then he pushed me back on the bed, jammed a pillow over my head, and started punching me. When I felt the blade of his screwdriver stab through the pillow and into my neck, I twisted away, rolled to the wall, slid down between the wall and the mattress, and dove under the bed.

The man couldn't reach me under the bed, and I curled myself into as small a ball as I could manage. I didn't know I was in danger of bleeding to death, I was just trying to avoid being stabbed or hit again.

He swore, jabbed at me under the bed, yelled at me, but he couldn't reach me. Finally, he gave up. I heard him run away and heard the backdoor slam shut. I waited, feeling the blood running down my T-shirt. After what seemed a long time, I crawled out from under the bed..

I went down the stairs, and as I passed my mama's hatchet, her defense weapon, I felt relief that the man hadn't seen it to use on me.

I staggered next door where my brother Kevin was playing Atari video games with the neighbor kids. I pounded on the door, a woman answered, saw me covered in blood, and screamed. I fell into my brother's arms as he sat on the couch, and he started screaming too, setting off a roomful of hysteria.

The ambulance was called, and I was rushed to the emergency room. Most of my family lived in those projects and word quickly spread to my mother, who was hanging out elsewhere in the flats. Mama arrived at the hospital shortly after the ambulance did.

"Don't say nothin' about what happened!" she warned me.

My mama had stolen money from that man, and because of my unconditional love for her, I never said a word. I understood what my mama did, how she needed to support her drug habit, and I knew how she also supported my brother, me, her sisters, boyfriends, and numerous friends to the best of her ability.

I understood.

I kept my mouth shut.

As I lay on the stretcher, I heard the paramedic tell the doctor, "This kid nearly bled to death. We got him here just in time!"

My stabbing started a roller-coaster of events over the next thirty-plus years, and they're still going on now. The nine-year-old boy is now a 40-year-old man who has weathered peaks and valleys, from a high of being a high school football star in a state where football is king, down to time in a solitary jail cell.

Despite the challenges and obstacles, I would, through God's grace and my persistence, be able to experience events that dreams are made of.

The past has nothing new to say, so I have learned to not listen to it. Yet, I shall never forget the uneven journey through the years, and lessons learned from this ongoing odyssey. My story, which has led to financial success, exoneration in the criminal justice system, and a new career in motivational speaking with creation of the TIKI Factor, continues.

I was born Wednesday, July 27, 1978 in Andrews, Texas. "Wednesday's child is full of woe" seems to be an accurate folk saying, for I would have my share of sorrow and pain mixed with joy and happiness. I was born prematurely, weighing just two pounds, and was so small that I slept in a dresser drawer when my parents brought me home from the hospital. My father, Frank Coulter, and my mother, Karen "Louise" Young, parted company shortly after I was born. Mama named me Tiki after a hotel and gave me her maiden name, Davis, as my surname. My middle name is Frank, apparently as acknowledgement of my parents' relationship.

Mama left me with my father, who also wasn't ready to take care of me. His mother, Grandma Hattie raised me until I was about four. Those few early years were the happiest and safest of my young life, and I wish I could remember more from that time. When Mama came and got me, I lived off and on with her and with her mother. Mama and I stayed in a variety of temporary places, often in motels or with other family members.

While being stabbed was scary and almost fatal, it was just

one of many traumas that happened while I was an on-again, off-again part of my mama's messy life. I became a petty thief, and as the song goes, when I fought against the law, the law usually won.

My education was a patchwork of dozens of different schools, where I struggled until I found a salvation of sorts when I was placed in foster care.

In foster care, I learned for the first time in my life there were actual rewards for doing the right thing. Good behavior, prompt attention to chores, cleanliness, and completing homework assignments earned weekly allowances and often weekend trips to amusement parks, movie theaters, and other fun outings. I even learned some salesmanship skills selling candy door-to-door, and that success in dealing with the public would pay huge dividends decades later.

I was introduced to Pop Warner football and through my God-given strength, speed, and agility, discovered my ability as a running back. Coaches noticed, too, and by the end of my junior season at Odessa High School, I seemed poised for greatness, ready for a standout senior season and already carrying numerous letters of inquiry from major college programs regarding where I might wish to run for a fully-paid college education and possibly a National Football League future.

During my last few years of high school, I finally had some stability with a wonderful foster family, Sam and Joyce Watts and their children, who treated me as one of their own. I had a sweet girlfriend, my own car, and to borrow another song's lyrics, my future was so bright I had to wear shades.

Those shades proved to be blinders, and an encounter derailed my senior football season and all those dreams and hopes. Although I was innocent of the assault charges leveled against me, more than 20 years would pass before my name was cleared. I spent six months in the Ector County Jail, missing my senior year in high school, and by the time I was released, my future seemed as empty as my pockets.

My mother was in prison for murder when I got out of jail, and we managed to have some time together at the prison for a long visit. It was the last time I saw her.

God works in mysterious ways, and at His chosen pace. Thank God He also placed a host of wonderful people in my life, including my foster parents, who remain an integral part of my family. After I received my high school diploma, I went to work at porter and car washer at Bronco Chevrolet in Odessa. I eventually worked myself into position to be a salesman on Saturdays.

Over time, I was noticed by the owner, Steve Late, who took a personal interest in my life. Eventually he said, "Tiki, if you pursue your dream, I will pay your tuition to any college in Texas. As long as you stay in school and make passing grades, tuition will be covered."

I enrolled at Sul Ross State University, about a two-hour drive away, and I did my best to make up for my senior year in high school. I'd strongly felt my year of football glory had been stolen from me, so I tried out for the football team. Though my teenage hopes of stardom were not realized, I was a running back with some playing time and I was thrilled to score a few touchdowns.

When a coaching change meant a change in my playing situation and I was benched, I quit the team. Still making up for my lost senior year, I decided to campaign for Homecoming King and won in a very close election. When I told a university staff member I had achieved my goals and was ready to move on, he stopped me cold with his response: "Yes, Tiki, but have you earned a degree?"

I considered my options, and I am convinced the voice of God reminded me that it was time to grow up; this wasn't meant to be a substitute for high school. It was time to think of my future.

I committed to school and dived into my studies. I also became involved in the university's theatre program and was active in the Black Student Association, Although I no longer was a student-athlete, I convinced several Odessa athletes to enroll at Sul Ross. I earned my bachelor's degree in 2003. I still was on probation for the assault charge and decided to stay in Alpine to work toward a master's degree as well. I completed the requirements two years later.

I had a real breakthrough about this time. I had given up my dream of being a professional athlete at age 22 so that I could focus on my education. I did not want to be a player on the field—I wanted to be a player in life. I made a total commitment to live from my imagination and not my history. They gave me a football and told me to run, but I took the time to educate myself.

Make no mistake, when you make great changes in your life, it will cost you your old life.

Outside the classroom and the stage, my life's journey continued to have highs and lows. My mother died in prison before my final semester of my undergraduate studies, and we sadly buried her on the day of her scheduled release from incarceration.

Shortly after graduation, I launched my movie career, first as an extra, then with a speaking role in *Friday Night Lights*, based on Buzz Bissinger's book about a season of Odessa Permian

High School football, and starring Billy Bob Thornton. The experience and friendships I established would position me for future encounters of the previously-unimaginable kind.

I made another screen appearance in *The Three Burials of Melquiades Estrada,* directed by and starring Tommy Lee Jones, but post-graduation life mainly involved oilfield employment boom and bust—lucrative pay and bonuses followed by layoffs. By then I was married with an infant daughter, and once again, I learned the Lord will not lead you where He will not keep you.

When my daughter was born, I searched for my dad, whom I'd not seen often in my life, and not at all since I was a young boy. I found him in a nearby state, built a relationship with him, and he's a part of my life and my daughter's now.

My long-time habits of keeping some get-away money handy enabled me to buy vehicles and equipment for a mobile car wash, and within months, my earlier car sales experience produced monthly income that approached what I earned in the oilfields. I parlayed my oilfield engineering skills into a successful consulting business, and soon my enterprises expanded into trucking, real estate, residential construction and two successful barbeque restaurants.

My entrepreneurial success earned me several prestigious business awards in the Odessa-Midland area, and I was a millionaire before my thirty-fifth birthday.

Despite numerous appeals to the court system to restore my good name, that cloud lingered over my head. I had achieved the financial success portion of the American dream, yet I felt something was still missing in my life. As Shakespeare wrote, "Who steals my purse steals trash . . . But he that filches from me my good name robs me of that which not enriches him, and makes me poor indeed" (Othello, Act 3, scene 3).

Through my church membership, I became a mentor to teenaged boys and young men, attempting to show them through my own experiences the possibilities available through making positive choices, but my life's work remained unfulfilled.

God once again took my hand and led me to Bishop T.D. Jakes' church, The Potter's House, a large nondenominational church in Dallas, Texas. When Bishop Jakes posed the question, "Are you chosen?" I believed that God spoke to me through his words.

I had been financially rich, yet spiritually broke. It was not until that moment that I knew what was missing: God. There are no paths to success that do not involve God.

Within the next two years, amazing things transpired. My 1996 accuser contacted my attorney and me, recanted the accusation, and through a court order, my name was cleared. I met motivational speaker Les Brown, who heard my story and became my mentor. I continue to travel as a motivational speaker, discussing **The TIKI Factor:**

T=*Total Commitment.*

I=*Imagination.*

K=*Kindred Spirits*, maintaining relationships with positive people with like-minded goals, ethics, and morals

I=*Invest in Yourself.* My story has attracted attention from both the motion picture industry and publishing world.

God has never left my side, guiding me from the depths of poverty to achievements and associations I would never imagined. God makes no mistakes and He directed me on a path that included hardship and heartache because He knew I could overcome. My story is not mine; it belongs to the world to share with others the possibilities available by grace through faith.

Biography

Motivational speaker Tiki Davis' journey of travail to triumph from the streets to the stage illustrates the determination of man coupled with God's grace through faith.

He attended Sul Ross State University in Alpine, Texas, earning a bachelor's degrees in communications, with a minor in theater, and a master's in liberal arts.

Using engineering experience gained in the West Texas oilfields, he started his own successful consulting business, and has interests in real estate, residential construction, and two successful barbeque restaurants. He was named Odessa's Black Entrepreneur of the Year and was also honored by the Odessa Chamber of Commerce. He became a mentor to boys and young men, telling of his trek through adversity and stressing the potential benefits of positive choices and good judgment

Tiki Davis shares his story and *The TIKI Factor* with churches, corporations, high school, and collegiate athletics teams, youth groups and organizations, and individuals committed to making a difference in their own lives and those of others.

Tiki still lives in the Midland-Odessa area, and he has one daughter, Brooklynn, 10.

Contact Information:

www.tikidavis.com

Facebook: @thetikifactor
Twitter: @thetikifactor
Instagram: @thetikifactor
You Tube: @thetikifactor

CHAPTER FIVE

There is No 'Secret' to Success

Marie Cosgrove

Imagine that at this moment you have everything of which you ever have dreamed. You have the perfect job. You have a perfect family. You have perfect health. You have _____ (fill in the blank). You are a success. Imagine your perfect life.

How would that perfect life be different than your current situation?

If you have all you've ever dreamed about, I suppose you *are* happy and fulfilled. And that's great news. Congratulations to you!

If you are not fulfilled and successful, what are you willing to sacrifice to get what you want? Would you be interested in knowing the secret to obtaining your every dream and desire as well as achieve massive success?

I am sorry to break it to you, but *there is no secret to success.* Despite all the webinars, books, and seminars promising to give you the "secret" to achieving success, you will not find it in some hidden message. You will not find it in a secret potion. You will not find it via a psychic guru, intellectual guru, or once-in-a-lifetime seminar.

However, if you keep reading, you will find one of the formulas for success.

One of my good friends, who recently performed his sold-out comedy act in the Selena Auditorium in Corpus Christi, Texas, laughed when he saw the headline about his act in the local paper: "Overnight Success."

The reality is that it took him years of discipline, determination, and dedication. Yes, that was his formula for success—**discipline, determination, and dedication.**

If you dedicate yourself to these three points, it is possible for you to reach massive success—even millionaire status. Let's review them in some more detail:

Discipline: Are you disciplined enough to do what it takes during your downtime to help you reach success?

For example, when I was a single mom of four young children, I took steps that would help me grow. When I say single parent—I mean it literally. The children's father lost parental rights. I had no child-support. No financial backing. No days off without the kids. Although being a single parent rarely gives you extra time, the downtime I did have I used to study and grow to advance my career. Eventually, I became very successful within the company for which I was working.

Determination: How determined are you to reach success?

Unfortunately, I was fired from the company in which I had achieved great success. Regardless, I maintained my determination to be a success. *Instead of becoming bitter, I decided to become better.* I had to reinvent myself and stay determined. I started a new career with another company and eventually earned enough to start my own company.

Dedication: Olympic Gold Medalist Jesse Owens said, "We all have dreams. But to make dreams into reality, it takes an awful lot of determination, dedication, self-discipline, and effort."

Imagine my shock at being fired after I had given up so much to reach a high level of success. I was the top national sales representative for the company that fired me. My dedication did not diminish when I was fired. In fact, instead of being diminished, my dedication grew stronger. Within two years and with much hard work, discipline, determination, and dedication, I bought the company that had fired me.

When I purchased the company, many in my industry predicted I would bankrupt it and myself within six months. Eight years later, we are still strong—proving that the three success principles—discipline, determination, and dedication—are the ones you cannot afford to ignore if you want to reach success.

Never Stop Learning

I am incredibly blessed to have been raised by my grandparents. My grandfather taught me important lessons that helped me reach success and that I continue to follow today: *Never stop learning. Always have a teachable spirit! You need to exercise your mind just as much as you exercise your body.*

He went on to explain, "The more you exercise, the stronger your muscles become. It is the same way with the brain; you need to feed it, use it, and keep it engaged. Always keep learning and using your brain because it is a muscle. Learning is something you just keep doing, whether you are a baby, or 100 years old, you will never 'know it all.'"

I recall the day my grandfather retired and sold his barbershop. The very same day he retired, he enrolled at the local college to keep his mind active and engaged for the same reason he walked to work every day—to keep fit.

My grandfather's barbershop is also the place where I developed my love of reading and learning. I would spend afternoons reading his comic-book collection and *National Geographic*. He gave a free comic book to every child who got a haircut. I always made sure I had read my grandfather's new comics before he gave them away.

National Geographic gave me an opportunity to "travel" the world. When I was a child in Texas, we did not travel outside of own large state. *National Geographic* gave me a glimpse into an entirely different world and an opportunity to learn about different animals, nature, and cultures.

I was reminded of my grandfather's words when I read a story about a time when one of the greatest artists of all time, Michelangelo, was asked to provide a talk on art at the age of 87. His reply was, "ancora imparo," which means "I'm still learning." Michelangelo had a teachable spirit and true humility.

As a 48-year-old woman with four adult children, three grandchildren, and a little one still at home, I continue on the path of life-long learning that my grandpa showed me. Along the way, I have learned some valuable lessons that have helped me continue.

Humility—Maintain a teachable spirit. Remaining humble is necessary to develop a sincere heart and a desire for learning.

Responsibility—Take the first step in learning. Being prepared to act when presented with new learning opportunities is assuming responsibility for your own growth and success.

Defeat—The greatest motivator for learning. I love the example of Benjamin Franklin; he was brilliant and loved learning, but his parents could not afford to keep him in school. He had to leave and go to work when he was only ten years old, but despite this setback, he persevered. He became an inventor, an author, and perhaps the most famous founding father of our beautiful nation.

Difficulties—Opportunities for learning. Looking back at my life, one of the greatest challenges I faced was being fired when I was the sole financial supporter of my household with four small children at home. My dire situation forced me to learn new skill sets and opportunities in a different field.

Maturity—Learning values. A mature person recognizes the need to seek wisdom and appreciates learning opportunities. In contrast, an immature person believes she is intellectually superior and places little value on continued education that may lead to advancement, growth, and success, essentially capping their full potential.

The Break Through gives you numerous examples of people who struggled through challenges and used the above five lessons in learning to succeed when they faced difficulties, loss, or defeat.

As you examine where you are in the five levels of learning, why not adopt *ancora imparo* as your motto? Dedicate yourself to accept and nurture learning opportunities that may come your way. Embrace the difficulties and defeats that will catapult you to new learning breakthroughs.

Legacy

What do you want your own legacy to be? Do the actions you take today leave a legacy to be carried in people's hearts for generations to come?

I vividly remember enjoying one glorious, warm autumn afternoon, highly unusual weather for Dayton, Ohio. I was in the car with my family and overwhelmingly happy.

Then the phone rang. My brother-in-law gave us horrible news. I went from overwhelmingly happy to overwhelmingly sad—emotionally going from zero to sixty as I heard my brother-in-law say, "Dad was diagnosed with pancreatic cancer."

The tears would not stop flowing. My heart hurt so deeply. My heart hurt for the entire family. I have been in the medical field for over 15 years—from what I know, pancreatic cancer has one of the highest mortality rates.

My youngest son was seven years old at the time. I could not picture him growing up without his grandfather—the only one he had left.

I have loving memories of my grandfather who helped raise me. I was fortunate enough to spend time with him throughout my entire childhood, and I learned my most valuable lessons from him, such as "never stop learning." I cannot imagine what life would have been without my grandfather; he made my childhood unforgettable.

I wanted my son to build lasting memories through his relationship with his grandfather, like those I was blessed to have with my grandfather.

We went to South Dakota the first opportunity we had to spend some quality time with my father-in-law.

I began to ask my father-in-law questions to learn more about him. I will never forget the answer to the question, "What is the one thing that you wish everyone knew?"

He said, "*Everyone* has an expiration date. Some of us know the date, but most of us do not. How you live your life *before* your expiration date is what matters."

He shared a story about an inmate who was on death-row and had accepted Christ. On the day he was to be executed, he had a huge smile. The other inmates asked him, "Why are you smiling? Don't you realize you will be executed today?"

The inmate replied, "All of us have an expiration date—except most of us don't know the date, but I do know mine! I am happy because today I meet my maker and savior!"

My father-in-law was also a man of faith. He had dedicated his life to serving others. He voluntarily gave his time freely to underprivileged, at-risk youth so that they can grow emotionally, mentally, and spiritually to hopefully break free from things that held them back.

Dolly Parton said, "If your actions create a legacy that inspires others to dream more, learn more, do more, and become more, then, you are an excellent leader."

My father-in-law also devoted his time to serving his family through his life's example and by giving them words of wisdom so they could be spiritually filled, leaving behind a legacy that lives on in the hearts of those he loved and onto a thousand generations.

There are some questions you can ask yourself to help you build a legacy you can be proud of for years to come. A legacy that will not only survive materially but also will survive in the hearts and minds of those you love after your 'expiration' date—an expiration date we will all experience.

What are the contents of your book?

My father-in-law taught me through the way he lived his life that *your life is your book.* What does your life look like in the chapters you have written?

What actions are you taking today that will impact the way people remember you? Will the actions you take today leave a legacy to be carried in people's hearts for generations to come?

I will always be thankful for the small gestures my father-in-law has shown me; they have left a significant impact on my heart. When I was pregnant with my son, he called me frequently to make sure my pregnancy was coming along well. He encouraged me when I was feeling 'blue.' He had an ear for listening. He took time away from running the farm to call his daughter-in-law, which showed me that he genuinely cared and valued me as a person. His actions showed me he had a kind, loving spirit.

What do you want your legacy to be?

You can make changes in the way you live your life today so you can leave behind a powerful, impactful legacy. You can determine *now* how others will remember you. Your legacy can be the most extraordinary, unforgettable, and valuable inheritance for those you love.

Biography

Marie Cosgrove is a successful entrepreneur with a proven track record of
turning failing companies into profit
centers. Among her successes is being
fired from a medical device manu-
facturer specializing in developing
devices to help doctors diagnose con-
cussions, traumatic brain injuries,
dizziness, and vertigo, to purchasing
this same company who had fired her. Eight years later, she
continues to lead this company and has taken it international.
She also grew a start-up medical device company specializing
in arterial and vascular diagnostic solutions into a 14-million-
dollar company within two years.

Marie has over 15 years' experience in the medical industry
where she closely works with top neurologists and medical
researchers on the brain's ability to rebuild neuropathways,
which until recently was thought to be impossible. A renowned
international speaker, she talks about how we can rebuild these
neurological connections, strengthen cognitive ability, and
"unleash the genius mind" that is inside us all.

She has shared the stage with motivational speaker Les
Brown and *New York Times* best-selling authors Brian Tracy and
John Maxwell. Marie serves on the Forbes Coaches Council
and as President of the Advisory Council for the John Maxwell
Team. She has been featured in *Hispanic Executive* magazine
and recently won the I Change Nations Golden Rule Award.

Marie is a Certified Facilitator Instructor in the Round Table Method, by Global Priority Solutions, Certified Human Behavioral Coach, Dr. Paul Scheele Learning Systems, 'Reclaim the Brilliance" Certified Trainer, Certified DISC Personality Profile Facilitator, Business Coach, and Trainer.

She is the founder of The Virtue Project, a nonprofit specialized in assisting single moms and troubled teens learn personal, professional, and entrepreneurial skills for success.

Contact Information:

You can follow Marie at:
www.mariecosgrove.com
Facebook: https://www.facebook.com/marie.l.cosgrove
LinkedIn: www.linkedin.com/in/balanceback
Instagram: https://www.instagram.com/marie.cosgrove/
www.thevirtueproject.org

CHAPTER SIX

Don't Break Down Before You Break Through

Donna Gates

Let us not become weary in doing good,
for at the proper time, we will reap a harvest
if we do not give up.
—Galatians 6:9 (New International Version)

When you feel like giving up, it's just time to ask God for His strength. At that moment before failure, you will discover you're truly at your strongest with His help.

You have to make up your mind to walk right up the mountain when problems arise ahead of you. Don't ask God to move the mountain, ask Him to give you the *strength* to climb it. There are no shortcuts. If He pushes it aside, that same problem will keep rearing up in front of you until you finally get enough faith, willpower, and strength to climb it with God's help.

Not all problems come from the devil. Some things you just need to endure.

At one point in my life, I was hooked on emotional pain. I despised my own life; my inner self had become my enemy. Pain was my normal, and I'd gotten so familiar with its constant throb that I rejected all forms of comfort. When I received compliments because I succeeded or people thought highly of me, I rejected them because I was sure those people were trying to hurt me.

I was publicly successful and powerful but privately miserable. I asked myself the question: *So many people are jealous of me that I must be doing well, so why do I despise my own life so much?*

I remember the day a light bulb finally came on for me and I understood the way I perceive things was stopping my personal development. I began to think my way out of self-doubt, just as I'd thought my way down into it.

A big step was when I decided to stop inconveniencing myself to satisfy other people. I quickly began to understand that everything I do from this point on will either build me up or tear me down. The trials of life had already cut me deep, so this was my opportunity to finally heal.

Life is 10% what happens to us and 90% how we react to it.
–Charles Rozell "Chuck" Swindoll

Just Land On Your Feet

Jabez cried out to the God of Israel, "Oh, that you would bless me and enlarge my territory! Let your hand be with me and keep me from harm so that I will be free from pain." And God granted his request.
—I Chronicles 4:10 (NIV)

When you ask God to increase or enlarge your territory, you're asking Him for more than real estate or money. You're asking Him to let you have more responsibility, more opportunity—to elevate you and increase your life so you can make a bigger impact for Him.

If you have ever asked God to increase your territory in any capacity, you may already know what comes with elevation. If you ask and believe, that is exactly what He will do, but I must warn you it will not come without trials and tribulations. There is a price to be paid. You will be tested in ways you didn't anticipate.

Let me explain; loneliness comes with elevation, confrontations come with elevation, betrayal comes with elevation, and enemies come with elevation. God will turn your test into your testimony and your mess into your message if you persevere. Your mistakes will be helpful when you look back and they're things of your past.

You must always remember: *It is only a test!* The harder the test, the greater the power. The test is temporary! When things are falling apart and you seem to be under the most pressure, your mind is the most creative and you will begin to think outside the box.

Go back to the drawing board and take advantage of this opportunity to invest in your goals so that you may grow through what you are going through. Go to a quiet place, away from distractions, so you can open up your heart in order to hear and receive God. Your adversities will benefit you if you don't give up. Remember, you already have everything in you that you need to be successful.

We must look for ways to be an active force in our own lives. We must take charge of our own destinies, design a life of substance, and truly begin to live our dreams.

—Les Brown

You Must Have A Sense Of Humility

For as he thinks in his heart, so is he.
—Proverbs 23:7 (New King James Version)

Humility is the opposite of pride. With humility comes wisdom. When you're humble, you're able to serve others, a key to personal development, and effective leadership. Being humble, you put aside your pride and get rid of your ego, because your ego will destroy you if left in place. You learn to be pleasant in unpleasant situations.

Being humble is to bring out needed characteristics for further growth, allowing you to gain balance in your everyday and professional life.

To be humble, you must be coachable, grateful, patient, dependable, disciplined, and able to recognize your own weaknesses. You must have courage, gratitude, endurance, enthusiasm, integrity, and most of all, faith.

Your thoughts become your reality, so now is the time to improve the quality of what you think. You're not any better than or worth any more than the thoughts you allow in your mind. Once you learn to sincerely and generously celebrate the accomplishments of others, many windows of opportunities will open for you. In return, you will become a more confident person and inspire others.

Faith Over Fear

Now faith is being sure of what we hope for and certain of what we do not see.

—Hebrews 11:1 (NIV)

Faith cannot dwell in the same space as fear. Faith is complete trust or confidence in someone or something. Fear is one of the most negative emotions and often leads to excessive worry and severe anxiety.

You must commit to yourself that you won't allow fear to control you. This is one of the key decisions that set me free from my pain and the way I'd lived most of my life. Sometimes, we hinder ourselves from other negative emotions such as being ashamed or full of pride.

If you want God to really heal you, you must get real with yourself just like the blind man in Mark 10:46. It's one of my favorite scriptures, so I'll tell you the story. A blind beggar heard that Jesus was coming down the road with a crowd of people, and he started shouting, asking Jesus to have mercy on him. The more that people warned him to be quiet, the more he shouted and asked Jesus to have mercy on him. The blind man was so persistent that he didn't care what anyone else was saying; he was hungry for his healing, and he knew only Jesus could help him.

Jesus stopped and called the beggar to come over. He asked him, "What do you want me to do for you?"

The blind man said, "I want to see."

"Go, your faith has healed you," Jesus said. Immediately, the blind man began to see, and he was able to follow Jesus down the road.

That's awesome! So, if all the blind man had to do was just call on the name of Jesus and have enough faith to be healed, then why do we keep going through the same fears and pains over and over again?

Way too many of us have allowed fear to attack us, and we live with it every single day of our lives. Fear can not only paralyze you, but it can sink you just like it did Peter in Matthew 14:22. As long as Peter had faith, he walked on water, but as soon as he began to fear, he sank like a stone.

Fear will stop you from doing the things you desire to do in life. I have seen that for years.

Picture yourself lying on your deathbed and seeing all of your dreams and visions surrounding you. Imagine them saying to you, "You could have given us life, but you allowed your fears to paralyze you. Now we must die." What has fear prevented *you* from doing?

What if I had never gotten over my fear? I would have never written this chapter, never purchased a home, never moved to a brand-new state, never started my businesses, never been successful, and never been happy.

Do any fears keep you from making an important decision?

God is coming to your marriage, to your relationships, your homes, and your work; He is going to restore your faith if you allow Him to enter into your thoughts to develop your vision and purpose in life.

Sow with an attitude of faith and expectancy. This will open doors for God to move on your behalf. Study and pray daily. Make your needs and desires known to Him.

Faith is a gift that is afforded to all human beings equally. Your current circumstances or situation don't make any difference; we all have the same opportunity to exercise our faith and believe in our higher power for what we can't currently see.

When you put faith over your fears and stop worrying about what people are going to say about you, you will not only excel in life, you will excel in Him.

My Child Saved Me

During one of the most trying and fearful times in my life, my daughter was my *why*—the reason I did not give up. I was young and afraid of being a teenage mother, and I reached an unimaginably high level of depression and stress. Having a child who depended on me to protect her was scary; the reality of what it meant to feed, clothe, and nurture this beautiful little girl made me tremendously anxious. As I tried to figure out what I needed to do to take care of my baby, my whole outlook on life began to change. My mind began to shift gears swiftly and I jumped into a protective mode for my child.

I never wanted my daughter to experience what I had endured as a child. I could protect her from some of what happened to me, but I had no control at all over other areas. I had to make a decision not to let fear take over and control me by allowing my present circumstances to determine my future.

Although my parents have always been very supportive of me, I knew that raising my daughter was something I had to do on my own. I needed to prove to myself I could do this—I *could* be a loving, supportive mother to my child, just as my mom has been to me.

As I grew as a mother and a woman, whenever I faced bad situations, I began to think and speak about winning at life rather than focusing on *defeat*. That was also when I decided to get serious about becoming an entrepreneur. Within two years of my child being born, I started a business, and it turned out to be very successful. Now I tell others, "Either build your own business, or someone else will build it and hire you to work for them. It's up to you!"

My business also allowed me to keep my child with me and not get a sitter. This was a wonderful benefit, and it meant far more than just the child-care savings. Our mother-daughter bond grew strong because of the limitless amount of time we spent together every day. If I had to raise her all over again, I would not change a thing; my child's happiness brought great joy to my heart. (It still does today.) Since she was born, her happiness has given me a reason to live and strive to be a better person.

It's not what happens to us, it's what happens "in" us when it happens to us.

—Johnny Wimbrey

Making Our Transition

But the one who does not know and does things deserving punishment will be beaten with few blows. From everyone who has been given much, much will be demanded; and from the one who has been entrusted with much, much more will be asked.

—Luke 12:48 (NIV)

We use affirmations to reprogram our subconscious mind, to help us believe things about ourselves and where we fit into the world. When I learned to speak affirmations daily, I began to grow and began to see an improvement in my finances, spirituality, health, and emotions.

Each morning when I wake up, the first thing I do is start speaking my affirmations:

God, I thank you for waking me up and blessing the lives of my family and friends. I am loved by you and I will look for signs of your presence and grace today.
No weapon formed against me shall be able to prosper.
I am the lender and not the borrower.
I am above and not beneath.
I can do all things through Christ who strengthens me.
I am in transition to be rich so that I am able to be a blessing to others and I will never be broke another day in my life.

We must make up our minds that we don't want to be just comfortable anymore and we will do whatever is necessary to get out of our comfort zones. We must change our environment, and usually need to change the people we hang around. We tend to find people who have the same problems we have because we want to be comfortable, but if your circle of people does not motivate you to grow and go to the next level, you are hanging with the wrong group of people.

If you allow other people's negativity to affect you, you'll be held back from moving forward. Make up your mind to be around people who challenge you to stretch beyond your dreams and find your *purpose* in life. Your *purpose* is that thing that you enjoy doing, that seems effortless, something you'd do for free.

Once you've found your purpose, expand, and build it by keeping your commitment to yourself. Educate yourself daily whether it be reading a chapter in a book every day, listening to an audiobook while driving, motivational videos, and searching out writings from people who inspire you. That is how you practice and exercise self-control.

You must develop a tremendous work ethic. You must challenge yourself daily in order to discover your true greatness. You are responsible for what you have been given whether it be wealth, talent, time, resources, or knowledge. You are expected to be a blessing to others. Most importantly, don't expect people to understand why you suddenly changed and why you are doing certain things differently.

You must be the change and break those generational curses that have plagued your family. We must teach our children they can do whatever they put their minds to if they stay focused and don't give up.

Let yesterday be the last day that you did not follow your dreams. No matter what you are going through or where you are in life today, you must do everything within your power today to make tomorrow better. Tomorrow is the first day of the rest of your life, so take advantage of it and start working toward your dreams, goals, and purpose every day.

It doesn't cost you anything to try, but it might cost you everything if you give up. Do not over-estimate the cost of greatness! Yes, you might fail, but how will you know if you never start? If you don't try, it's guaranteed that success will never be one of your options.

Biography

Donna was born in the Mississippi Delta area in the small town of Shelby, and she attended school in nearby Clarksdale. Her grandfather was an old-school Baptist preacher in a small country church, and because of him, she had a spiritual upbringing. Donna said, "We sure knew how to worship God in that small, non-air-conditioned church!"

In 1990, she developed an entrepreneurial mindset and a yen for a big city that led her to Wichita, Kansas, where she lived for seven years. When she decided to go bigger, she relocated to a Dallas suburb, Carrollton, Texas, where she lived for 14 years before moving back to Mississippi to be closer to her parents.

When she lived in Kansas and Texas, Donna met many of her goals and milestones, owning and operating child development centers and selling real estate. In 2009 she finally had the resources to accomplish her biggest dream, launching a charitable organization. She's the founder and CEO of Share A Life Foundation, Inc., a 501(c)(3) non-profit organization that focuses on helping the homeless, underprivileged families, and finding transitional housing for them. She also owns a home health agency, National Health Care LLC, that services the Mississippi Delta.

Donna has one daughter, Ala, and she lives in Jackson, Mississippi.

Contact Information

Email: iamdonnagates@gmail.com
Website: www.iamdonnagates.org
Facebook: www.facebook.com/iamdonnagates
Instagram: www.instagram.com/iamdonnagates
LinkedIn: www.linkedin.com/in/authordonnagates

CHAPTER SEVEN

Never Give Up!

Marco Da Veiga

I am sitting in a coffee shop in Oslo, working on my book, writing to you. Why?

Because I have faith that I can help you, and I believe the Almighty Creator will lend a helping hand.

As I write this, I see I have had a lot of victories and breakthroughs in life. My failures, though, have given me wisdom; wisdom has taught me patience, and patience has given me the gift of hope. Hope has made me greater, better, and stronger.

Whenever we travel to reach one objective in the series of goals we set for ourselves, we can easily visualize that we are traveling from one mountaintop to the next mountaintop.

What's important to understand is this: *Between every set of mountaintops, there is a valley.* The valley is tough; this is where your character is tested and you will be pushed to your absolute limits. You will be forced to bring out the best in yourself so that you can overcome the challenges and reach the next peak.

Yea, though I walk through the valley of the shadow of death, I will fear no evil; for You are with me; Your rod and Your staff, they comfort me.—**Psalms 23:4, New King James Version**

On your journey, you always need to acknowledge God and

His presence. He will help you stay focused and keep a good attitude, because there is no room for distractions in the valleys.

Let's talk about valleys.

One of my valleys was a very deep one. I resigned from a job I loved and in which I excelled to go into business with a woman I had met in church. She spoke confidently about her contract with international brand makers and said she was working on a collaboration with Europe and the United States.

I pulled on my gloves and went to work with her for free. I sold my house, my BMW, and went all in. I uprooted my son Marcus and we moved to where my new partner lived. I promised I would help her for six months on this project and help her restore another company as I worked on a new project of my own in Morocco.

Though I believed in my business partner and what she said, as time went by I realized I'd been deceived. Everything about her was a lie and an illusion. My mistake was being too trusting in her as an individual and not researching her well enough. I realized that what I thought was the truth was not true.

I had made a big mistake.

Even though I was in the valley, this experience reinforced my belief that we should always build good relationships on trust, manners, and honesty. I continued to make good connections with new people as I traveled to Germany, London, and Turkey on this doomed business.

I was in a good place, but with the wrong partner. Finally, I had seen what I am capable of doing—running three companies at the same time, working late, waking up early, and doing what needed to be done while I built relationships. It was time for me to be on my own. After five painful months, I left.

Though I felt I was in the wilderness, I followed up on my

new contacts and relationships. After careful thought, I decided to move ahead with my Turkey-to-Morocco clothing import business.

I can do all things through Christ who strengthens me.— **Philippians 4:13 (NKJV)**

My travel to Turkey increased to two or three times per month and trips to Morocco were even more frequent. I set up my company in Agadir, Morocco, negotiating with the bank director, who became a great friend of mine, and going to the court to set up the structure of the company—and did all of this in French.

I tell you, I had to hold on to the word of God and trust Him like a child holds on to his parents. I cannot explain the trauma, pain, and mental toughness it took to survive and sustain myself.

Cast your burden on the LORD, And He shall sustain you; He shall never permit the righteous to be moved.— **Psalms 55:22 (NKJV)**

I had invested nearly $40,000 in setting up my new business, after everything was done and told with the costs and traveling. Six weeks before my shop was supposed to open, all was looking well, everything was organized, the logistics and customs were in order. I was on a mountaintop.

Then, disaster. Morocco increased the tariff on clothes coming from Turkey by 50%. All of my profits were gone, lost. I had to pull out before the loss became even greater, and for the next two months, I traveled back and forth between Norway and Morocco to make sure the shutdown and all cancellations of contracts went smoothly and legally.

I suffered a great loss and my mind was just boiling. "I lost it all," I thought. The choices I'd made put me in a tough situation, and I was doing all I could to maintain the right attitude, to believe in myself, and to push forward, but honestly, I was drained. It's as though I'd been poured out like water.

It is good for me that I have been afflicted, That I may learn Your statutes.—**Psalms 119:71 (NKJV)**

I had to make some tough decisions, and I did, and I stand behind them and take full responsibility. I made mistakes, but if you don't take risks and make mistakes, you will not succeed. So, to those who are reading this book, *stand strong and keep marching forward.*

There are beauty and love in the results of my failure and mistake.

This is the beauty: If I had stayed at my job, I would never have sold my house and cars. I would never had been able to travel with my son to Dallas, where he was baptized at the Potter's House, and where I was baptized again.

This is the love: I never would have had the opportunity, chance, or time to travel to Nigeria where I met my best friend, now my beautiful wife, my Princess. (By the way, Princess is her real name.)

My journey of hardship, experience, pain, tears, and the endless travel to England, Turkey, Morocco, and Nigeria, made me reflect. Finally, I understood that it all had a reason and a purpose.

This is why I say: *Never give up.*

I give God all the glory for this great breakthrough, for His faithfulness and loving kindness. I would not have made it without my Lord and Savior Jesus Christ.

Every good gift and every perfect gift is from above, and comes down from the Father of lights, with whom there is no variation or shadow of turning.—**James 1:17 (NKJV)**

Believe in yourself, push toward the goals and dreams you have, *just be prepared,* because life will inevitably mow you down at some point. Keep God close by your side at all times. And while no book or audio can completely prepare you for the blow, a good background in personal development, reading, and sharpening your skills will give you a chance.

I am a living witness. I am living my dream, fulfilling my purpose, but *only because I was threshed and humbled.* I grew by being stretched and pulled into uncomfortable and even unbearable positions—but look at me now! I made it and I broke through.

Recently, I was in Lagos, Nigeria, where I hold workshops on leadership and management for Nigerian youth. The university in Lagos is supporting my charitable organization, and as I write this, we're finalizing our business plan and budget. I will be able to reach and inspire young people in a country with more than 100 million people under the age of 30.

This has been a lifelong dream, and despite all the setbacks and pain, I have never been happier or more fulfilled. In life we learn so much every day. All the experience we gain from it—good or bad—is priceless. Now there are a lot of ways to prepare oneself, to get ready and tackle the challenges and difficulties that may come along your way, and I am going to share my best with you.

The Big Five States of Mind

Use these states of mind to prepare you for your walk through the valley and the wilderness as you journey from mountaintop to mountaintop.

Before you start, understand there is no difficulty greater than your capacity to solve it. Remember, you are never alone.

Faith. *You must have faith;* it makes all things possible. The

Bible tells you that faith can move mountains, that you only need faith the size of a tiny mustard seed, and that everything is possible for he who has faith, for all things are possible for God.

Whether you believe in God or not is not the point—*faith* is the point!

Believe in *yourself*, have faith that you *can* and *will*: Yes, you must reach your goal, you will finish your task, you must make it on time, things will work out for you, and you are going to make it!

Though I can't begin to express how important it is for you to have faith, I ask you to trust me and follow me on this first of the big five daily disciplines—have faith.

I ask you to trust me and I will not lead you astray, for you are my brother and sister. Have faith!

Hope. I love hope, because when things are really difficult, I always hope; I say to myself, *Everything's gonna be all right.* One of the world's greatest musicians ever, Bob Marley, says it beautifully in his song "Three Little Birds" when he tells you to not worry about anything because *every* little thing will be all right.

Yes, hope for the best. When your hope is combined with faith, you'll really know that every little thing *will* work itself out. You still might have to fight and stand firm for what you want, but hope will keep your head above water, always!

Please trust me here, too, and take this sweet mellow vibe called *hope* to your heart. Use it in your life to overcome your challenges, for you are greater than any wall that blocks you!

Love. Love is the greatest state of mind. Love caused the creation of all things—that's why we're here. Love makes the world function!

When you carry love in your heart and learn to love yourself in truth and in spirit, you can then love your neighbors. You're a master of humanism and on the path of righteousness.

Sometimes it's hard to love because you're afraid your heart will get hurt, but don't let this stop you. Learn how to protect your heart; use your experience to know when and how you should open your heart to others. In any case, you can still love.

I don't know who you are yet, but I love you. I want the best for you. I support you in all that you do as long as your deeds are good and positive.

If you can love me, and I love you plus all the other seven billion people in the world, then I am asking *you* to *also* love the seven billion others.

Why? Because there is something in them that is similar to the thing you love about me. So find it, be humble, and love and respect each other. At least don't hate or fight, even if you can't get along.

I am asking you to trust me, embrace love, and use it as a guide and force in your life. (Don't forget to teach your children how to love, for charity begins at home.)

Positive. Positivity is a game changer, and I can't emphasize enough how important it is for you to be positive. When you are in a positive mental state of mind, you become unstoppable. Being positive is being on another vibration and on a higher frequency! A righteous man's vibration is always positive.

It took me some time to grasp the full depth and importance of being and staying positive.

I have had a lot of ups and downs and I've encountered challenges as I was moving from one mountaintop to another. By being positive and telling myself with faith, hope and love *#everything is gonna be alright*, I got through whatever it was

I had to go through. In every case, my experience became a life changer.

So smile and be happy even when things are really hard. Dig down deep in your soul and give thanks for whatever you are learning. As I said earlier and I'm happy to repeat, *There are no difficulties greater than your capacity to solve them.*

Decide now that you are going to be a positive person! The effect it's gonna have on your life and those around you will be fantastic, but there's more than that. Positivity is also energy that you as a human being send out to this world and universe.

If negative friends or family members pull you down, drain you, and give you less then you give back to them, don't spend as much time with them.

Either you change your friends, or you *change* your friends!

Wake up and live! Be a positive soul, be part of the positive vibration!

Optimistic: I love to be optimistic; it just makes me feel good to have a mindset that things will always work out, that after rain comes sun and through darkness comes light.

Inhale and embrace this thing we call optimism and use it in your daily actions; carry it in your heart.

I know the first time you read this book, you may stop, contemplate the five states of mind, and say, "Yes, I'll give one or two of them a shot." That's not enough. I ask and beg you to make every one of them a *habit*, because when you become a master of the Big Five, you will really feel alive.

Practice these daily disciplines and make them a part of your lifestyle so that you will be a good human being. These mental habits will give you the strength and courage you need to keep pushing for whatever it is you want in your life! Remember, this is *your* life and you can design it however you want.

It's not always gonna be easy to reach your goal, but it sure is possible. Trust me when I say that the Big Five will help you get there, they will make you get there!

The only way you can lose in anything in life is if you give up! *Never give up!* Be an optimistic person. Say out loud, *I am going to make it!*

Say it again: . . . ***I am going to make it!!!***

Biography

Though Marco's family is from the Cape Verde Islands, he was born and raised in Norway. During his childhood, Marco suffered discrimination and harassment; he credited his survival to his strong belief in God.

As he matured and continued to fight against the forces of hate and intolerance, Marco evolved into the leader, teacher and entrepreneur he was born to be. He's a graduate of University of Oslo, where he studied early childhood and youth work.

Marco began his outreach by founding Youth United after an apprenticeship in African Youth in Norway, OMOD and Antiracist Center. He's ambassador of Youths Against Violence in Oslo.

He is the Norwegian rap champion, beginning his recording career in 2005, when he released his first single and music video. In 2008, the music video "O.D. 98" was showcased on MTV, The Voice TV and other media as part of a CD compilation, *Let Me Be Heard.* He reached the semifinal of *Norway Got Talent in 2011,* with an original song that he wrote to his son. In 2012, Marco played Bob Marley in "The Legends" at the Norwegian Opera & Ballet and Nordic Black Theater.

He has performed and given talks in South Africa, Sweden, Nigeria, Denmark, Trinidad, Senegal, Cape Verde, the United States, England, and Norway on TV, radio, and in many locations.

Currently, Marco is the CEO of both Youth Nation, a charitable organization with a mission to *"Restore faith and hope through leadership and management,"* and a consulting/teaching company, Born to Inspire.

Marco is married to Princess, and he has a son, Marcus. He divides his time between his work in Nigeria and his permanent home in Norway.

Contact Information:

Marco Da Veiga
Mobile: (+47) 40469602
Email: mdvunited@gmail.com
Instagram: @marcodaveiga
Twitter: @marcodaveiga
Facebook: www.facebook.com/marcodaveiga
www.marcodaveiga.com

CHAPTER EIGHT

你 做 得 到
(You Got This)

Stacy Ho

In 2016, I was sitting in a van, heading to the airport. With a breaking voice and tears in my eyes, I said, "You know, I always thought I would be the wife of a Rotary President. I never thought it'd be me as Rotary President."

"Stacy, you've done well," Past President George assured me.

The certainty in his voice went straight to my heart. I never thought I would be the hero of my story. I always imagined playing a supporting role.

My story starts quite unassumingly.

Ten years ago, I lived in a perfect bubble. I was raised in a wholesome loving family of seven. My parents had five children and I was in the exact middle.

At this point of my story, I need to tell you that my mother is an amazing woman who is kind, loving, emotionally supportive, and the greatest mom in the world. I do not mention her a lot here because this story is about my father and what he taught me. I am fortunate and grateful to have had two tremendous parents who shaped me into who I am today.

My father was an entrepreneur. He was magical. He

was a fighter. My father grew up as a tycoon's son. Due to a combination of inopportune business choices and post-war market conditions, my grandfather lost his wealth and never recovered. My father told me that my grandfather was only 50 years old when he lost his wealth. My father did not understand why his dad could not find it within himself to rise again. As a result of experiencing the rise and fall of my grandfather's business empire, I believe my father developed his phoenix personality.

A phoenix is a magnificently feathered mythical creature that dies and rises from the ashes—born again from defeat. My dad always told me he was a phoenix. When we experienced low times in our family business, my dad would put on a smile and a fighting spirit and head out to the world. He had a saying that went, *"Another day, another way! We must keep on going! And never say die!"*

Unfortunately, I speak of my father in the past tense because he left this world in 2011. His death was the hardest period in my life.

I was twenty-four when my dad was given a three-year prognosis. Receiving the news from my parents was so unreal. It was the biggest shock of my life. Words. Words. Words.

Words like:

Multiple Myeloma.

Terminal cancer.

Rare.

Incurable.

No proven treatment.

Three years.

The news hit me hard.

I would be losing my loving father, best friend, mentor,

boss, soundboard, and so much more. I also would be losing all my imagined/planned future possibilities for my life.

My game plan for my life was to be my best and work for my family. I would be taken care of forever. School fees, allowances, salaries—everything until that point—had always been provided to me by my father. I was my father's princess. The apple of his eye, his pride and joy.

My dad was *amazing*; he was a visionary. He was a loving doting father. He put us all through good schools and did whatever he could to provide us a great life. He had big business deals and then he had bust business deals. We had our ups and we had our downs.

My dad believed in himself.

My dad told me a story about the most powerful Chinese words he ever heard. When my dad was a budding entrepreneur, my grandfather said to him, "你 做 得 到."

你 you

做 do/work

得 obtain/get/possible

到 reach

Independently these four characters are simple, yet the combination of the four when delivered encompasses un-wavering faith and belief that "you" can do this. In modern day vernacular, the equivalent of 你 做 得 到 is: "You Got This!" My grandfather's words fueled my dad to achieve his first big break.

My father never doubted his ability to spring back from anything. He would never give up. If there were any setbacks in a project, he would say, "Okay, now is the time to retreat and re-strategize so that we can re-launch."

When we had virtually no business, no customers, no

clients, and no meetings, my father would take us to open house events of huge luxury homes. He would take us to showrooms for luxury automobiles and allow us to sit in the different models and accompany him on test drives. He would take us to different trade shows at exhibition halls. He would spend hours talking to us about his big dreams and all the wonders we all could live and experience together.

That was my dad.

In 1999, we were on the brink of bankruptcy. At one point, we were so broke that we were counting our pocket change to make sure my brother and sister had school lunch money. My dad never gave up. He kept on fighting and looking for opportunities. He kept on working on possible deals. That very same week, he closed a million-dollar deal. By 2004, we were once again living in a large luxurious 5,000-square-foot home with two cars, a chauffeur, and housekeepers. My dad showed me the magic of being a phoenix.

"Stace," he told me, "Aim high. Dream big. Never give up. Always keep on walking."

Dreaming BIG was a characteristic and value my father drilled into us.

Before the news of his cancer, I planned everything. I was a total control freak. I had planned my entire lifetime. I planned when I would finish my MBA, when I would meet the love of my life, when I would get married, what our wedding would be like, how many children we would have, and at which age I would give birth to each of our children.

At every single milestone, I saw my father.

I always planned that life would be my dad and me, side-by-side, building our empire, because I was the *best* personal assistant/right-hand man in the world. I was my father's lieutenant.

你 做 得 到 (YOU GOT THIS)

The saddest moment was realizing I could not have those moments with my father. I felt lost and hurt. I was mad at myself for having the audacity to plan such a beautiful life.

My father battled cancer for three years. In that period, we moved from Bangkok to Hong Kong so he could enroll in a university clinical trial using stem cells to treat Multiple Myeloma. My father truly believed he would become that rising phoenix one more time.

Unfortunately—this time around—being a phoenix was not in his cards.

෩ ෩ ෩

Perhaps the biggest casualty of my father's cancer and eventual passing was the death of my vision, hope, and passion.

I became a zombie.

I went to work, ate food, sometimes hung out with friends, slept, and repeat. Work. Food. Socializing. Sleep. Repeat. Every day, every moment was about just going through the motions.

I had been my father's apprentice since I was 14 years old. He trained me how to be a successful respectable responsible entrepreneur. Immediately after his passing, however, I could not face running my family business.

In those years, just seeing my dad's handwriting would make me choke up and cry. It killed me not to be working on our business; but without my dad, I did not know how to show up in the business world. I always viewed myself as the supporting cast, not the star.

I did not have the heart nor the passion to revive our family business, so I did the best I could do to earn money to support my family and that was private tutoring. I taught one-on-one private coaching lessons for subjects like Business Studies,

Economics, Mathematics, and SAT Test Prep to high school students. My students bring so much joy in my life.

My big breakthrough happened when I hit rock bottom after three years of living in zombie mode. I was incredibly proud of my students—seeing my them graduating high school, moving on to university, starting their lives—I felt left behind. They were moving ahead by leaps and bounds and conquering the world, whereas I was stuck in the mud.

That awareness brought several months of total despair that was irritating and painful because I *knew* I had to keep on living. I *knew* I had to force myself to get out of bed and as my father always taught me, *"Just keep on walking!"*

However, *'keep on walking!'* just took way too much energy.

On the second anniversary of my father's passing, I could not get out of bed; I could not manage taking even a sip of water. That was June 24th, 2013. On June 25th, 2013, I had to teach a student who lived two hours away from my home. That student was bright, happy, and enthusiastic about achieving her goals. I knew I had to show up for her because that was my commitment: to prepare her to excel on the SAT. I could not get out of bed for myself, but I made myself get out of bed for her.

That two-hour journey was hard.

Throughout the whole commute I kept telling myself, *"left foot, right foot, left foot, right foot."* I knew I had to take that journey one step at a time. As my father taught me, *"Keep on walking. Tomorrow is another day, never say die!"*

Step by step.

Just kept moving. Just kept walking.

Through this, I learned that tiny steps add up to big steps. Infinite steps mean distanced covered. Just keep on moving.

你 做 得 到 (You Got This)

❧ ❧ ❧

Change happened when a close friend attended an Access Consciousness® class. She learned of a healing technique called *Access Bars®*. My friend gave me a session as a gift.

After the session, I felt different.

To this day, I cannot pinpoint exactly what I felt different about. I dug further by watching YouTube videos (of Access Consciousness) and exploring Access Consciousness materials online. I went on Amazon and bought and read sixteen of the books before attending my first class! I enrolled in a four-day workshop titled, "The Foundation." At that time, the course fee was relatively hefty for me—$1,400. However, I knew I needed to get the necessary tools to recreate my life. So, I saved up the money for the class. In the end, someone 'paid it forward' and I received the workshop as a gift. How does it get any better than that?

By day three of the course, I was not feeling much of a shift. That was the moment I forced myself to get uncomfortable, be vulnerable, and really look at what was working for me and what was not.

The biggest breakthrough I had was learning I did not need to be the provider. I did not need to take on my father's role. The act of "taking care" of everyone was in fact crippling my family. I was being the superior asshole who thought I was the only one who could earn money. I never gave my siblings a chance to stand on their own feet and support themselves.

For several years, many friends and family members had encouraged me to stop looking after my family and start focusing on *my* life. It hurt me every time I heard the words: *'Stop providing for your family. You are not your father.'* I worried,

85

"How could I abandon ship? How could I be so selfish? What is the meaning of life if not providing and taking care of my family?"

What I realized is that choosing to be a provider was never a position my family imposed on me. It was a role I "bravely" took on because I thought it was my responsibility to do so.

The idea that I could choose for myself and live my own life was scary. I never had made myself a priority in my life. Coming out of that four-day workshop, I felt like I was embarking on a journey to an uncharted frontier. I felt so lost. I did not know in which direction would I go?

"Stacy, what if your vision is not clouded and murky? What if instead you have a whole sky of infinite possibilities ahead for you? You have no more anchor points and you are totally free to choose anything you would like. In this case, what would you like to create?" Dr. Dain Heer, co-Founder of Access Consciousness, encouraged me in one class. In other words, Dain gifted me with an illuminating perspective: I had a blank canvas in front of me.

In another class, Gary Douglas, the Founder of Access Consciousness, gave me valuable advice:

"Stacy, go back to the basics. What do you love? Start from there. Spend time observing people, and if you see anything you'd like to have in your life, start asking for similar."

So that is what I did. I spent time reading books, studying the lives of iconic people, meeting and speaking with people from all walks of life. After a while, I had an idea of the life I would like to create. Within 18 months, my whole financial reality changed: I built two new businesses; I became a Certified Facilitator with Access Consciousness, and I traveled to different cities to teach "Five Days of Change" workshops. It was amazing. Furthermore, my relationship with my body changed so my health made a big turnaround too.

From this breakthrough in my life, I learned *we* give our lives meaning. Life can be meaningless or it can be meaningful. It is up to each of us to discover what meaning we pour into life. What would be fun to create? What would make life worthwhile? If there were absolutely no limitations, what wildest inconceivable dreams could we make real?

ໜ ໜ ໜ

When my dad was in the ICU ward, I excused myself and went out to the hallway. I sat on a chair. Broke down and cried. I could not let my dad see me like that because I thought I had to be strong and positive in front of him. To my surprise (and horror), while I was crying, I saw my dad walk out dragging along his IV machine—he was looking for me! He was shocked to find me crying.

He sat down beside me and asked me why I was crying. *"Is it because you are worried I'm going to die?"*

I guess he knew me too well.

"I don't know what to do," I told him. "I don't know what to do if you go."

Foolishly, I was crying about him as if he already died—even though he was right in front of me. He pulled me in close. Locking eye contact with me, my dad took my hand gave it a firm reassuring squeeze and spoke.

"Stace. 你 做 得 到," he said.

I was too grief-stricken to appreciate the gift he gave me in that tender moment. As if he was passing on the baton: those words were meant for me from now on.

你 做 得 到

(You can do it.)

我 做 得 到
(I can do it.)
I can do it.
I got this.
And I am doing this.

Now that I have achieved success, I understand why he said those words. He had always treated me as a princess, provided for me, looked after me. I had no inkling as to what I could truly do on my own. I always thought life would be handed to me on a beautiful platter.

Right now, my life *is* on a platter—a platter designed, prepared, and cooked by my very own hands.

And what a beautiful platter it is.

你 做 得 到 (You Got This)

Biography

Born in Montreal, Canada, Stacy had a nomadic upbringing. As the daughter of a serial entrepreneur, she grew up and went to school in Hong Kong, Bangkok, and Singapore.

Stacy graduated with the Top Student Award and First Class Honors from the Manchester Business School where she obtained a Bachelor of Science (Hons) in Management, and she has a Bachelor of Science (Hons) from the London School of Economics in Accounting and Finance.

Stacy finds teaching to be an absolute joy. She tutors her students in academic subjects and teaches them strategies and skills to help them master subjects and gain lifelong confidence. She also teaches life tools through various workshops, empowering people to realize they can create the life of their dreams.

Stacy is very involved in community service and is an active member and Past President of her Rotary Club and Guider for her Brownie Unit. She resides in Hong Kong.

Contact Information:

Email:
stacy@stacyho.tv

Facebook:
www.facebook.com/stacyho

Instagram:
www.instagram.com/stacy_ho

Websites:
www.stacyho.tv
www.sheroesclub.com
www.improveyourgrade.com

CHAPTER NINE

Let Me Be Your Greatness Coach

Tony J. Reese

We can change the world by helping great people discover their great gifts and talents, and by helping them discover the great work they're meant to do. I know this to be the absolute truth: Every person on earth has been blessed with powerful gifts from God, and we are meant to use them while we do the great work He has planned for us to do. You must accept this truth, too.

My own breakthrough to freedom came from serving and helping great people—people like you. Have you heard the "greatness coach" used as a job title before? That's my job. My goal and mission are to identify and help you water your seeds of greatness so you can serve and change the world with your great work.

Zig Ziglar said if you help enough people get what they want in life, then you will always have everything you, yourself, want in life. This is the law of sowing and reaping. As we pour ourselves into other people, God will reward us. That is how we will break through and change the world.

So, why am I partnering with Johnny Wimbrey, Les Brown, and the other great authors in this book?

My mentors taught me to hang around people who are doing what you aspire to do, people who have been there, done that, and are still doing it. Johnny and Les are doing the things I want to do and they're attracting the type of people I want to serve. They help to bring out the greatness in me, and I am grateful to both of them. I also became their *Break Through* co-author because I want to change the world by helping you walk in purpose, lead in the areas of your giftings, and learn to solve the problem you were born to solve.

Simon Sinek's *Start with Why: How Great Leaders Inspire Everyone to Take Action* is a powerful book to read, and I recommend it to you. When we start with *why*, our *what* becomes more impactful and people will connect with us on a more emotional, deeper level. Emotion causes motion; connecting with people on the heart level gets them into motion. Leadership is serving and loving people in the areas of your giftings. Leadership is influence. Leadership means inspiring, influencing, impacting, and imparting your great gifts into others to help them live a breakthrough life.

What you are most passionate about, what pisses you off, what are your past pains, previous experiences, and what do you like to practice—all of these things are tied to your purpose and the problem you were born to solve. As you figure out how to connect all of these things—and get paid for your efforts—this will eventually become your great work.

Let's move to *you*. Let's figure out what your *why* is.

That which
you love

Passion   Mission

That
which
you are
good at

★

That
which
the world
needs

Profession   Vocation

That which you
can be paid for

★ = Purpose

What is your "why?"

- What are the great gifts God has blessed you with?
- What problems were you born to solve?
- What are you most passionate about?
- What pisses you off?
- What past pains or problems have you been able to get through?
- What is your potential?
- What previous experience gave you a snapshot into your future?

As you start answering these questions, you begin to identify your why, your purpose, and the problems you were born to solve. Once we begin to fulfill our purpose and start to solve the problems in our communities that we were born to solve, it's time for us to enlarge our scope to encompass our state, then our country. When we all are fulfilling our purpose, we'll eventually change the world. The world's problems will start to decrease, and the world itself will be changed for the greater good. This is how we can all breakthrough together.

I do not believe in coincidences. I do believe all things work together for our mutual good as long as we keep the right attitude, or PMA—a Positive Mental Attitude. I believe you are reading this book because you want more in life and you really want to help other people discover more in life.

My Gifts and Breakthrough

We breakthrough by telling our stories. I want to inspire you by telling you how I broke through and share some keys to help you with your own breakthrough. If just one person is inspired by my breakthrough story, then I am walking in my purpose and helping to solve one of the problems I was born to solve.

Over the years, I've worked to know myself, to understand my gifts. Now I know my biggest passion is people, and I can, with a level of sophistication, relate to all different types of people. My great gifts are positivity, creativity, connecting people, and serving them in leadership. I love leadership development, and to me, to lead is to serve.

My unique genius is helping to connect people's great gifts and talents to their great work, work that's centered around their purpose, and the problem they were born to solve.

I'm passionate about people and believe economic injustice is one of the problems I was born to solve because I grew up in extreme poverty. I relate to Johnny's first book, *From The Hood to Doing Good*, because I lived in places like Johnny's—some

One of the Greatest Injustices

We've almost forgotten one of the greatest injustices and tragedies that has happened on American soil, and since it's hardly ever discussed, I thought I should bring it up here.

Almost 100 years ago, hundreds of black people were massacred and thousands were bombed in their prosperous segregated neighborhood of Greenwood, part of Tulsa, Oklahoma. This was just a couple of hours from where I was born and raised in Oklahoma City, not in the deep South as you might expect. At least 300 black people were killed and 800 treated for injuries, but only 36 deaths were listed on the official reports at the time. The neighborhood was known widely as Black Wall Street because it was so wealthy.

I ask you to Google Black Wall Street and learn about the bombs dropped from airplanes, and how a white mob was allowed to loot and burn the neighborhood with tacit permission from city officials. In the wake of the violence, 35 city blocks lay in charred ruins, and thousands of its residents were locked in detention camps. What we had been building, fresh out of slavery, was destroyed. This was a legal and economic injustice that pisses me off and I want to help make right.

of the most economically challenged government-funded neighborhoods in Oklahoma City.

My dad was accidentally killed when I was three years old, and my momma became an alcoholic, battling depression the whole time I was growing up. She was violent and abusive with my two younger siblings and me whenever she got drunk. Once our family started receiving welfare, government housing, and food stamps, we became dependent on them and that was the norm for the people we lived around. I started to believe there was no way out of this system once we became fully dependent on it. Our environment controlled our mindset!

In most of these government housing projects, there were no men around and I believe that was intentional. Whenever the authorities discovered men were living in a home, the entire family would be kicked out of their subsidized apartment or house. And the more babies you had, the more money and food stamps the government would give you. This injustice is still happening in 2020.

One of the keys to my breakthrough happened when I was 16 and began to read the Bible. By that time, I'd already experimented with drugs, alcohol, sex, and gangs, and was traveling on the wrong path. My aunties Ilene, Sharon, and Bobby took me to Estes Park Church of Christ, where I met Jesus. I was saved and baptized, gave my life to Christ, and started to attend church on a regular basis.

God told me He would be my Father and directed me to Romans 8:15:

The Spirit you received does not make you slaves so that you live in fear again; rather, the Spirit you received brought about your adoption to sonship. And by him, we cry, "Abba, Father." **(New International Version)**

This is an extra-special scripture to me because my birthday is 8-15, and like Jesus, I am God's son, too.

The first thing we must breakthrough is our mindset.

Having a breakthrough mindset will put you on the road to breaking through *anything* that gets in your way. Before you change your mindset, though, you must give your mind new information. In my case, I started to believe what the Bible said about me and started confessing those promises over all aspects of my life. My mindset and my life were changed.

Church also helped me because it put me around positive people, which was key to my breakthrough. Once you're around positive people, you must change your environment and shed all the negative people you'd been hanging around with before.

You also need mentors who are always honest, open, and transparent with you (remember the acronym H.O.T.).When my basketball coach and mentor Tommy Griffin (father to NBA superstar Blake Griffin) told me I was not going to make it to the NBA, at first I was mad at him because I had major hoop dreams; I was sure basketball was my way to break through and get out of the hood. Then Coach Griffin gave me an alternative; he told me I was very smart, and if I focused, my grades would be my way out.

Richard Garrett, my social studies teacher, reinforced my coach's message in a very positive way when he wrote a letter to my counselors and the principal, saying I should be in advanced classes because I needed the extra challenge. I really appreciated Mr. Garrett because he saw more in me than I did at the time.

I also listened to my aunties, Ilene and Sharon, who were both school principals and gave me good advice. They also inspired me to get good grades because they paid me money for every "A" I earned. High school was where I met Odessa, who became my sweetheart and has been my wonderful wife for more than 18 years. Odessa always believed in me, spoke words of greatness to me, and prayed for me.

I also owe a big shout out to Rodney Porter, a mentor who was like a godfather to me. He kept me out of trouble during my high school years and drove me hundreds of miles from Oklahoma City to Greensboro, NC when I left for college.

I broke through because there were great people in my life who truly believed in me. I focused on getting perfect grades, became valedictorian of my high school graduating class, and was awarded a series of scholarships for college, including one from the Bill and Melinda Gates Foundation. In fact, there was enough scholarship and grant money to move my mother and younger brother to Greensboro, North Carolina, with Odessa and me.

When we breakthrough, we always should take others with us. The phrase *Each One Teach One* will help you remember this: If each of us teaches and mentors at least one person through the breakthrough process, the results will grow and multiply exponentially.

Know yourself

Before you can grow yourself, you must know yourself—

John Maxwell

The following will help you learn to focus your mind as you discover your own gifts and will put you on a path to discover your purpose:

- What do you believe about yourself?
- Are you walking in fear or faith?
- Were you created for a purpose?
- Do you have great gifts?
- In what area are you called to lead?
- What do you love to do?
- What do you believe you can do?

Having a Mindset Shift: Changing Your Paradigms

Paradigms are the way we experience, perceive, and interpret the world and its events, though we're usually not aware of how greatly they affect us.

One of the best examples of how paradigms affect our attitudes is included in the excellent book, *Riches for the Mind and Spirit: John Marks Templeton's Treasury of Words to Help, Inspire, and Live By.* I'll paraphrase Templeton's story about the Middle Ages: A man is sent to a building site to discover how the laborers felt about their work. The investigator approached the first worker and asked, "What are you doing?"

"What, are you blind?" the worker snapped back. "I'm cutting these impossible boulders with primitive tools and putting them together with the way the boss tells me. I'm sweating under this blazing sun, it's backbreaking work, and it's boring me to death!"

The investigator quickly backed off and retreated to a second worker, and asked the same question: "What are you doing?"

The worker answered, "I'm cutting up these big chunks of rock, which are put together according to the architect's plans.

99

It's hard work, but I earn enough to support my family. It's a job. Could be worse."

Somewhat encouraged, he went on to a third worker. "And what are you doing?"

"Why, can't you see?" exclaimed the worker as he lifted his arms to the sky. "I'm building a cathedral!"

Now, that's the joy of doing great work that you are passionate about!

Today, begin to look at your life as though you are building a cathedral. You're going to be both the architect and the stonemason. You are clarifying a vision of what your life looks like and your rules for worry-free, happy, and inspired living.

Create a vision of what your life looks like as you build it and when it is finished.

- What do you want in life?
- What are your heart's desires?
- What type of legacy do you want to leave?

Create a set of personal guidelines for living your life.

Begin with a set of guidelines for living an abundant life, guidelines that will tell you when you are on course and when you are off course.

List the strategic results you hope to accomplish in the next 12 months.

List your core values. Self-discovery is the most empowering time in your life. It's worthwhile repeating: In order to grow yourself, you must know yourself.

What is the contribution you want to make in the world? This is the part you play in assisting others to find their great work and water their seeds of greatness. Martin Luther King Jr. once said, "Life's most persistent and urgent question is, what are you doing for others?"

What is your unique genius? I describe this as the knowledge, skills, feelings, and beliefs you experience when you are operating at your God-given best.

Two of the greatest times in a person's life are when they were born and when they find out the purpose for which they were born. Let me inspire you, coach you, and help you to bring out your greatness, find your great work, develop your great fruit, and serve it to the world! Let's grow!

Grace and Peace!

Biography

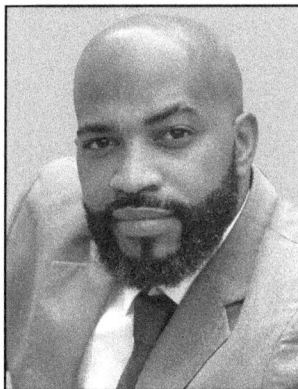

After graduating from John Marshall High School in Oklahoma City as valedictorian of his class with a 4.0 GPA, Tony and his high school sweetheart Odessa moved to Greensboro, N.C., where he attended North Carolina A&T State University and she attended Dudley Cosmetology University. They married while still in college and both graduated on schedule, Tony with a B.S. in Computer Science and Business Entrepreneurship, and Odessa with a Cosmetology license.

Tony and Odessa settled in Arlington, Texas, to raise their family, close to their Oklahoma hometown. Tony was working for a large consulting firm when he and Odessa founded Marriage4Real, a marriage and family coaching business designed to encourage and inspire couples through the many tests and trials that marriage can often bring. Their company inspired Tony and Odessa to publish *Prayers for My Wife*, and *Prayers for My Husband*.

With the publication of *Break Through*, Tony has launched a coaching and consulting firm to help others breakthrough, helping great people and great companies get their great work to the world by helping them realize the greatness within.

Tony and Odessa have been married 18 years and share four wonderful kids, Tobias Jeremiah, Taniyah Joy, Titus James, Trison John, and their fifth baby on the way—Truth Justice Reese.

Contact Information

Email: tony@tonyjreese.com
Websites: Tonyjreese.com
marriagefourreal.com
LinkedIn: Tony J. Reese
Facebook: TonyReeseRealEstate
Instagram: @tonyjreese

CHAPTER THREE

Obsessed with Money

Chelsea Galicia

I am obsessed *with* money. Personal and business finance, the economy, investing, and money in politics consume most of my working hours.

Don't misunderstand me, please. I am not obsessed *over* money. That's a very different path—a dangerous path—to take. Money alone can never make you happy, and I learned this truth the hard way.

By the time I was born, my parents' rags-to-riches story was well past the raggedy part. My mom had encouraged my dad to open up his own law firm in Los Angeles, and during my early childhood he grew his business while my mom worked and went to school part time.

When I was 10, my mom graduated from college with a degree in business administration and accounting. As soon as she passed the CPA exam, she went to work at my dad's law firm.

By this time, we lived quite comfortably and were looked after by a rotating staff of fulltime housekeepers in a home that my cousin called the pink White House. There would be other homes too—one that we stayed in every other summer for our vacations on Maui, one in the local mountains for skiing, one by the beach, and another on a golf course in the desert.

My mom felt it was important for my sister and me to understand where she came from—a dirt-floor home in Guaymas, a Mexican fishing village. Every year, my family would make the 16-hour drive so that we could give out used clothes, shoes, and toys to the people of the poor town where my grandfather lived.

My parents wanted us to understand what life was like for many people on the planet and to appreciate what we have. It worked—maybe a little too well. I took it to a level that probably no one intended. Yes, I felt grateful for my indoor toilet (just across from my very own Jacuzzi bathtub), but I also felt guilt for having so much when others had so little. Why was I so lucky? What had I done to deserve the good life that I had been born into?

The only honest answer was a whole lotta nothing. The only way I could reconcile my unearned good fortune was to live a life that honored my parents and helped others. So I saw it as my obligation to do well in school—that was important to my parents—and to show others and myself that I did not take my blessings for granted.

I did well in school, even though I hated every minute of it. And I did well in gymnastics, too; even though I loathed many minutes of it, because my parents liked that I did gymnastics. And as for career plans, I would honor my parent's work and legacy by becoming a lawyer and one day taking over the law firm they had built. In making this suggestion for my life, my mom explained that only a lawyer could own a law firm and so if no one in the family was a lawyer and something happened to my dad, we'd be forced to sell the firm. And, for dramatic effect, she added a white lie: "And we would lose everything." So with that, and a condo in Hollywood to live in, I was off to law school.

Until I passed the bar, I worked summers and part-time at my dad's firm doing depositions (questioning of witnesses under oath). As soon as I took the bar exam, I went full-time and shortly thereafter was given my first caseload, though I still didn't know if I had passed. (I did!)

Everything was looking good. I was a licensed attorney going to court, taking depositions, managing a caseload, and settling cases. The plan seemed to be on track. But soon enough, I couldn't shake the feeling that something was not right, that this was not right for me.

Part of the reason that this work had appealed to me, aside from honoring my parents, was that the work itself was honorable. I would be fighting for the little guy, an injured worker, against the big, bad insurance company who was denying him (or her) financial support and medical care needed to recover from an injury. The reality was disappointing, though not because most people are faking an injury. That kind of fraud happens less often than most people believe.

The real disappointment was with the legal and medical system. The kind of medical treatment people were getting was unhelpful at best, dangerous at worst. People were being pumped full of pain medication and under treatment regimens that seemed to benefit the doctors and pharmaceutical companies more than the patient.

I was furious with doctors and insurance companies for denying or delaying medical treatment, which prolonged pain and suffering, and sometimes required more invasive procedures than if the condition had just been treated right away.

I would be livid at how defense attorneys were incentivized by their compensation structure to drag out cases and create long drawn out battles when they were completely unnecessary.

The judicial system disappointed me, too. Sometimes a judge would be lazy and simply refuse to move forward with trial on the day it was set for, after all the work and waiting.

Then the compensation was often indefensibly, ridiculously small. After all the disastrous medical treatment and outcomes, the years of battles with the insurance company, the dismal compensation that people would get for life-altering injuries was just absurd, and it was my job to tell clients that this was all that they were entitled to under the system.

On top of that, I knew that my clients were in no position to handle the tens of thousands of dollars that they would be receiving in a lump sum. Mix human nature, my clients' level of education, and their often dire circumstances into this mess, and you can bet they'd run through their entire settlement in no time, making the whole massive effort an exercise in futility.

I wasn't really helping these people in any meaningful way, and there was no way I could make a real difference in their lives in my capacity as their lawyer. The system was broken. It was slowly beginning to dawn on me that this work was sucking up my energy and my sense of meaning.

When I looked ahead, I saw this would be my life from here on out. I had worked so hard in high school, college, and law school to get here. My parents had spent so much money on my education and supporting me for 25 years until I finally fulfilled their dream and became a lawyer.

When I took over the law firm, my parents could take more time off and ultimately enjoy retirement, as they had left their crowning achievement in the hands of the daughter they had so meticulously groomed. This was how I would support myself and sustain the high standard of living that had come to feel normal. This is how I'd be part of a rags-to-riches story, because I certainly didn't have one of my own.

To make matters worse, I began to realize that my dad, who for most of my life had been like my best friend, was not the man I had believed he was. I am grateful to my father for the immense support, financial and otherwise, that he provided me growing up, but for reasons I will keep to myself, I lost respect for him.

In short, he had become the epitome of the stereotype that gives lawyers their bad rap. Money had become everything to him. I do not mean to imply here that I discovered illegal activity on his part; I'm talking about his values and how he treated others. He wasn't truly happy, and he was taking it out on people around him.

And then he filed for divorce after 26 years of marriage; now there was no family or family business that I needed to protect.

All signs pointed to me getting out. The voice in my head repeatedly said, "This is not my life." Even episodes of Oprah (whom I have come to consider my third parent ever since I started watching her in college) seemed to warn me to leave and then affirmed my decision to walk away from it all.

One episode in particular validated my choice. Oprah's guest was Tom Shadyac, who is best known as a movie director for Jim Carrey movies like *Ace Ventura: Pet Detective.* Tom was on the show to talk about his documentary *I Am,* and he explained what led to making the documentary: He had achieved the pinnacle of success in Hollywood, had money and homes everywhere, was jetting around the world in private planes, and had tons of adoration, but ultimately he felt no happier than he was before these accomplishments.

Tom had done everything "right," but in the end, it felt so wrong. He came to ultimately ask the question, "What's wrong with the world and what can we do about it?" Through his documentary, he set out to answer those questions and share the wisdom he gained.

Even though I had achieved nowhere near Tom's level of success, I related to him. I related to the feeling of having everything in the world that you'd think would make you happy and knowing that it didn't. I too felt like something was very wrong with the way our society is driven toward "success," but couldn't articulate what it was. Tom and his film gave me a gift, the understanding that yes, being rich did not mean I must be fulfilled by the money alone.

Deep down, I knew a path of strict financial success would lead me straight to an empty and meaningless existence, as I had seen it do for many rich people around me.

In early 2010, I gave my notice, and had no idea what I'd do next. A friend who also worked in his dad's worker's compensation firm offered me a job, and I took it on a freelance basis. I decided I'd support myself by taking depositions while I figured out what I wanted to do with my life.

It turned out to be a great arrangement and a fantastic new business. Word got around and soon enough I was doing depositions on behalf of a handful of workers compensation attorneys. I worked part-time and made even more than I earned at my dad's firm working full time, and traveled, traveled, traveled. One year, I went to Turks and Caicos three times!

I joined a travel club and discovered an amazing opportunity to travel with an organization that built schools out of trash-stuffed discarded soda bottles in Guatemala. Over just three years, I went to work in Guatemala six times.

Meanwhile, my mom was settling into her retirement from the law firm. She decided to start a non-profit organization so she could help people experience financial stability and security by becoming skilled in dealing with their money, and named it the Financially Fit Foundation.

My mom knew that many people, even those who look successful, struggle with money, feeling like they never have enough. She could show them that their financial state was not a reflection of how generous their boss was toward them or how the economy was doing, but of their financial habits and their relationship to money.

About a year into her venture, she realized how much she preferred a behind-the-scenes role, and she recruited me to lead the workshops for the ever-growing crowd that met in her living room.

We created the curriculum together and I began to lead the workshops—and I loved it. Teaching was totally my thing—*this* offered the kind of difference I wanted to make in people's lives, and it turns out that I'm pretty good at taking dry, complex concepts and making them understandable and entertaining. I'm proud to be effective at helping people to become confident with money, and then show them the tangible steps to take that make it happen.

Our curriculum doesn't tell people how to spend their money. We help each person clearly understand their own values and goals and become aware of how aligned their spending has been (or not!) with those priorities. Then I show them a system that allows them to get their spending, savings, and investments on track with what truly matters to them.

Working with so many people has led me to a profound observation: Most people believe they're unhappy with money because they don't have enough. *They're mistaken!* What really makes them unhappy is that they spend inconsistently with who they think they are or what they want to stand for. In other words, they spend inconsistently with their values.

Of course, people need to cover the necessities, even ones they don't really like, but there is a method to spend and save in a way that honors who you are and what you value. This makes your money a tool for your happiness rather than a weapon of suffering.

In my own life, I am most satisfied when I spend time and money on items and experiences that reflect my values. In part, my obsession with money is a commitment to my values and a desire to live in accordance with them. I am by no means perfect or entirely consistent, but for the most part, I notice how much peace and ease I experience when I'm living according to my values. Aside from teaching, this provides me the most meaning and fulfillment.

Values have become the center of my work.

Let's be clear: I'm not talking surface values such as "I value fast cars and fine wine." That's just ego. I'm talking about deep values based within your character, integrity, and self-knowledge. Learn what makes you, personally, content and fulfilled.

The lack of values (or lack of clarity of our values) is what makes most of us miserable over money and drives us to spend more, more, and more, hoping to find fulfillment.

Living a life that honors your values is the key to your happiness. Now is the time to determine what those values are. Waiting until you become rich will, by my experience, make it less likely that you figure out what they are (unless you go through a personal or professional tragedy that breaks you).

It seems as though having lots of money and "stuff" can be a big distraction, and you'll find it even harder to look within yourself. Not to mention the "yes" people who let you believe what you say and do is acceptable and even brilliant, just so they can enjoy the perks of being in the rich person's orbit.

Let me add this: *Values cannot be bought. They do not arrive through a bank deposit. They are found through your investment into personal study, reflection, and discovery.* Of course, your values may evolve over time; what is important is to remain conscious of what they are throughout your life.

Keep clear about your own worth as a person so you don't slide into the trap of deriving your worth from money. Without your values to keep you anchored, you'll start to feel superior to those with less—and inferior to those with more. While you may feel different, you're not any better or worse than you were before you had money. Oprah says that money just makes you more of who you already are (and of course she's right!).

Any success story, including a rags-to-riches journey, is not complete until your prosperity is matched by your inner wealth, and you feel fulfilled, whole, and content. (You'll know you've succeeded when you're kind and honest with yourself and others.) The road to your inner wealth is paved with values, not diamonds.

There have been many excellent studies into what makes people happy and live long, fulfilled lives. The experts agree on *connection, contribution, purpose,* and *physical activity.* Of course, they mean different things to different people (yoga is a bit different from a triathlon). How do *you* interpret these four keys to happiness and a long life? What are the ways *you* want to experience them? How do *your* values express them?

Figure this out—it's worth a great deal of effort on your part to get it right—then make sure you spend more of your time and money on what you identify as your values than on what matter less to your wellness and happiness.

Remember this about your values: Look for them in what you buy, offer them in what you sell, and embody them— *live* them—as *what you are.* This is what trips most people up: it's only possible to do so if you are firmly grounded in the recognition of your own value and worthiness.

If there's only one thing you take away from me, it's this: I implore you to invest your time and your money into overcoming any negative self-worth issues you may still have. Most of us, including me, need to do this inner work.

Don't be afraid to ask for help, including therapy; don't worry that feeling good about yourself will kill your drive for accomplishment. It doesn't work like that.

I promise you—being happy is the best incentive for success you can have.

Biography

Chelsea is a financial coach and business consultant to millennial entrepreneurs, helping them create financially strong companies with values-based budgets, systems, and cultures. As director of education at the Financially Fit Foundation, she leads personal finance workshops for teenagers and adults. She is also a commercial real estate investor and shows others how to invest.

A progressive commentator and regular panelist on the weekly political podcast The Trump Report on AfterbuzzTV, Chelsea spends much of her airtime arguing that our fundamental problem is the role of money in politics.

Lawyering is her side hustle.

Chelsea graduated from the University of California, Irvine with a B.A. in Social Ecology, received her J.D. from Southwestern Law School in Los Angeles, and has learned enough from Oprah to have earned a Ph.D. Chelsea can't wait for the day that she finally meets her.

Contact Information:

www.chelseagalicia.com
www.financiallyfitfoundation.org
Instagram @chelsea_galicia
Twitter @chelseagalicia

CHAPTER ELEVEN

Learning
the Hard Way

Ralph Harper

I was born in the South, in tumultuous Birmingham, Alabama, in the early 1960s. I lived my childhood in the era when Birmingham competed with Jackson, Mississippi, for the title of ground-zero of racism.

My parents, my nine siblings, and I lived in a small four-room house in Ensley, a small town just west of Birmingham. Erected in a designated flood zone, our brick house was strong enough to withstand the storms, tornadoes, and the guaranteed spring and summer floods. The front yard was just big enough for a few of us to throw a ball back and forth or play "red light/green light." The back yard was bigger but weedier, and because we did not have a fence, stray dogs frequently visited us.

All twelve of us coexisted with plenty of love in our tiny home. During the day, the front room was designated as our meeting place; at night, it was our parents' bedroom. It was furnished with a sofa bed, a coffee table, two end tables with lamps, and the family television, which sat on a small table in a corner. The aluminum foil attached to the antenna was supposed to enhance the TV's reception; however, a few punches to the side of the unit seemed to work better.

Momma worked at the Catholic church in downtown Birmingham. She took the bus each day and returned home exactly at 5:32 p.m. if the bus was on time. At least one hour before we knew she would be getting home, we were careful to ensure the house was clean and all of our chores and homework were done.

I recall standing outside the house watching for the silhouette of her white uniform dress as she gracefully walked from the bus stop and across the school yard at Councill Elementary school where we all attended. Her presence was my reminder to get my act together. If any of us had gotten in trouble over the course of the day, we were sure to be spanked.

After dinner was cooked and eaten, we all gathered in the front room to share small talk and maybe watch some TV. When night fell, the moment when the bed was pulled out from the sofa converted our living room into my parent's bedroom, it was time for sleep. We kids had a bedroom with two bunk beds where eight of us slept and another small room belonged to my two older brothers.

Our house was not much to brag about; but it was our home. For as long as our parents were alive, we had a lot of love—some of it tough love—and three meals per day. My father, Clyde Harper, was a little laid back. He seemed content to come home from his job at the Post Office, buy a pint, and consume it before he went to bed. He was not the primary disciplinarian in our home; that was my beautiful mother, Mrs. Catherine Louise Harper. My friends in Ensley called her "Miss Hoppa," and they were afraid of her.

One day when I was just eight or nine years old, all notions of momma's fearsome disciplinary tactics were put into perspective and reduced to what I considered a simple slap on the wrist.

On a brisk, sunny Saturday morning around 9 a.m., my close friend Bobby showed up at my house. For a while, we played with a rubber ball in the front yard, throwing it back and forth. Then we decided to take a walk—an ill-advised walk—that turned into an hours-long extended tour of our neighborhood. We never told our respective parents of our plans. We just went on our way and returned about six hours later.

We stopped at Bobby's house first. His mother, Mrs. Murray, came outside and met us on the porch and she was very upset. She screamed and cursed us in between bouts of scolding and preaching about how worried our families and the neighborhood folk were. Finally, Mrs. Murray spoke directly to me. "Ralph—you know better! Catherine is gonna beat your ass when she gets home. Yeah, I called her already."

I was reluctant to face the music when she got home, so I decided it was safer to follow Bobby and his mother into their house. Inside, Mrs. Murray continued with her tirade. Suddenly, she screamed, "Bobby—take off your clothes!"

Bobby started crying, and he didn't move. Mrs. Murray became even more forceful in her tone.

"Boy—*take off your clothes*! I'm *not* gonna tell you again!"

Bobby finally took his shirt off, exposing his skinny torso, and Mrs. Murray told him to lie across the coffee table in front of her. Bobby was reluctant, and his cries grew louder as the tears flowed down his face like water from two faucets. He begged his mother, "Please, mama, I will not do it again."

I was scared and confused, and I began crying too as the scene escalated. Mrs. Murray glared at Bobby.

"Boy, you *better* lay across that damn table like I told you!"

Still crying and begging, poor Bobby slowly followed her instruction and stretched out on his stomach across the coffee table, knees touching the floor. Mrs. Murray, mumbling and cursing under her breath, took a few steps toward an open door, reached behind it, and retrieved a long brown extension cord from the doorknob. As she returned, still cursing, she wrapped the end of the extension cord around her right hand with her left hand.

As Bobby watched her every move, his cries escalated into horrifying screams.

Then the unthinkable happened. Mrs. Murray, a tall and powerful-looking woman, drew her arm back, and, seemingly with all her might, whipped her son on his naked back with the extension cord.

The screams from Bobby's mouth were unlike anything I had ever heard before in my life. I had never been so terrified. As Mrs. Murray drew her arm back again to administer the second lash, I could no longer bear being there another minute to witness Bobby's brutal beating.

I ran away as fast as I could, and I didn't slow down when I hit the front door. I did not touch the steps as I shot right off Mrs. Murray's porch.

I was in full stride, running because I felt my life depended on it. My hands were like blades, cutting through the air. My thumbs were pointed straight up to the sky; my head was tilted back with my nose pointed upward at a forty-five-degree angle. I was flying and I never looked back.

When I turned the first corner at full speed, I experienced a sense of solace in my heart. I was headed home, and I knew my punishment would not be anything like what I had just witnessed at the Murray house.

Today, that experience, that imagery, those sounds of screams, the tears, and that level of so-called "tough love" serve as the foundation for my belief that certain ills of slavery were passed down from the 1860s and may still be with us today. In my childhood, beatings far too often replaced structured discipline, teaching, and planning for the future.

In my case, when speaking of planning for the future: I was too busy trying to be Super Fly to think about *my* future when I was in high school. Oh, I worked; I started working at Prince Hall Apartments when I was a freshman. On occasion, I even gave momma a little cash to help with the bills.

However, I spent almost all the money I made on cheap clothes and shoes. I guess I wanted to feel like I was somebody important. I wanted to be noticed and popular. I wanted to be the "somebody" our elderly neighbor, Mr. Joe, had told me I would be someday.

When I graduated from high school, I was planning to attend Talladega College, but then I had a rude awakening. Even though I had worked steadily for four long years, all the way through high school, I was flat broke. I was broke because I consciously made bad choices and misused the money I made. I had no one to blame but myself.

Somehow, through the strength of my mother, the support of my father and my siblings, and a nudge from my high school biology teacher, Mr. Samson Julius Bennett, I was able to turn my life around and enroll at Talladega College, a historically Black college started in 1865, majoring in business administration with a minor in computer science.

During my junior year, I was selected for a summer internship at Equitable Life Assurance Company in New York City. The flight to New York was my first, and the experience of being in Midtown Manhattan was quite a cultural shock to a small-town Alabama student, yet I thrived on the experience.

Whoever oversaw the company's internship program was remarkably wise and very aware that small-town youngsters on their own in New York City for the first time could use some security and structure in their off hours. The company assigned me to a four-man dormitory suite at Columbia University, and my stay on campus was a major highlight of my internship (and most probably kept me out of quite a bit of trouble).

At the end of the summer, I returned to Talladega College to finish my studies. When I graduated, I was discouraged by a series of disastrous interviews for jobs in my home town, so I was surprised to learn the folks at Equitable Life were still interested in a Southern boy with a funny drawl. They wanted me to return to New York full-time; I was happy to return and relieved to spend the next eight months safely back in the Columbia dorm as I assimilated to city life. My next safe shelter, as I continued to save money for a place of my own, was staying for a while with the parents of a good college friend.

Figuring out how to survive and thrive in New York led me to my first venture into entrepreneurship.

I was dating a beautiful woman from Belize who loved to dance, especially on the Circle Line's jazz trips. Their boats circumnavigated the island of Manhattan, offering great music and a phenomenal view, but the rides were not cheap and I knew I couldn't afford to take my girlfriend as often as she liked. When I figured out I could charter the entire boat for $3,200 and I could sell tickets and keep the difference, it was a win-win opportunity. Each time I chartered the boat, I netted close to $8,000 profit and helped jumpstart my New York future.

After two years at Equitable Life, I landed a job at PepsiCo in White Plains, in suburban New York. I started at PepsiCo in an Information Technology Analyst role and worked on the national IT network infrastructure. Before I left, I managed some very large national projects, some with budgets in the tens of millions of dollars.

PepsiCo has an unshakable commitment to diversity and inclusion, and I did my best to support its progressive policies. I hired a variety of people, often people like me. After thirteen years, I transferred to Plano, Texas, to work at PepsiCo's Frito-Lay division, where I continued to manage national projects.

In 2001, I left PepsiCo to start my own company, DPLOYIT Staffing. DPLOYIT has been good to me and our employees. Over the years, DPLOYIT Staffing has placed thousands of employees and generated tens of millions of dollars in revenue in the process.

I am still CEO at DPLOYIT and the principal owner. But that is not enough for a full life.

Despite my perceived success, I know I failed in many ways. I failed because I was forced to learn the hard way—on the go and by chance, sinking while I learned to swim. No one ever gave me the answers to the questions I did not know yet to ask.

A few years ago, I had my eureka moment when Pastor Edwards of One Community Church in Plano, Texas, covered "purpose" over a month-long series and I finally discovered my purpose in life.

My purpose in life is to give this generation of our children the answers up front—early in their lives when it will make a difference for their future.

Since its birth, our country has missed the mark in terms of assuring children across all racial and socioeconomic groups are equipped with the skills and values they need to succeed in the United States. The issue has been perpetuated by two unsustained factors: finances and accountability.

One of the best examples of unsustained financial support is the digital divide impacting children in low-income families—the millions of children who have little to no access to technology.

When it comes to accountability, we can no longer ignore parents' unwillingness to properly prepare and guide their children; their unwillingness to give children the moral, ethical, and disciplinary tools they will need to be happy, functional, and successful adults.

Despite my success in business and my personal life, I know I succeeded only by random chance and lots of luck. This is my absolute biggest regret. If I had been prepared to seize my chances, I could have accomplished so much more! Mentoring would have made a tremendous difference in my life.

My God-driven purpose in life is to ensure children do not miss their chances and their possible successes the way I did. My mission is to ensure millions of underserved children across the United States will learn to live by the following seven **REWARDS** life principles. These life principles are embedded within three broader **WIN** accountabilities:

Workforce Development:
- Reading on a regular basis
- Education as the priority
- Working and appreciating the value of working very early in life

Integrity:
- Accountability for one's choices
- Respect for one's self and others

Next Generation:
- Duty to support the next generation of children
- Saving money and being financially astute

Imagine millions of underserved young children who live their lives according to the REWARDS life principles. When they make it to the 2060s, they will be educated, working, entrepreneurs, wealthy, Fortune CEOs, on corporate boards, politicians, and president of the United States of America. They will be the leaders of this country. So how do we help?

I founded Catherine Harper for Keepers (www.ch4K.org), a nonprofit organization named after my mother that focuses on four pillars: Fatherhood/Family, Mentoring, STEM, and Jobs.

I am a huge fan of Malcolm Gladwell and his "outliers" concept and have adopted his idea of ensuring our proteges will get 10,000 hours of IT training before going to college. I have many ideas on how to track them across several areas and assist them with getting jobs, scholarships, and other concepts.

Ideally, we will have CH4K Mentoring/Technology Centers erected in strategic locations around the country. While we still have work to do, we are growing our mentoring footprint in several cities around the country.

In 2012, I met President Obama at a small business conference at the White House. When I told Valerie Jarrett about my nonprofit and our seven life principles, she suggested that we work with My Brother's Keeper (MBK), a mentoring organization that was part of the White House initiatives. I returned to the White House and met with Broderick Johnson, who heads the alliance, and we are now connected with MBK, which is now part of the Obama Foundation

It is all possible.

So—let's go to work.

Biography

Ralph Harper was born and raised in Birmingham, Alabama, and earned a degree in Business Administration with a minor in Computer Science from Talladega College in Talladega, Alabama. He has held a number of IT leadership roles at Fortune 100 companies including Equitable Life, PepsiCo, and Frito-Lay. Throughout his career, Harper has been responsible for proposing, planning, developing, delivering, and supporting enterprise-wide technologies with multimillion-dollar budgets.

He is currently Chief Executive Officer at DPLOYIT Staffing and Business Solutions, which he founded in 2000. In 2008 and 2014, DPLOYIT was recognized by INC, Magazine as one of the fastest growing companies in the United States.

Ralph is Chairman of the Board and founder of Catherine Harper for Keepers (CH4K), a nonprofit organization which is aligned with President Obama's "My Brother's Keeper" initiative.

A motivational speaker on topics ranging from business strategies to fatherhood and the plight of underserved children, Ralph is also the author of an upcoming book that details a plan to improve our children's life outcomes (the working title is *Own the Change—The Mission to Bring a King's Dream to Fruition*).

Contact Information:

Ralph Harper
PO Box 659
Addison, TX 75001

email: shawn@ralphharper.com

Web Addresses:
Company: www.DPLOYIT.com
Non-profit: www.ch4k.net
Personal: www.ralphharper.com

Instagram: mrralphharper
Facebook: Ralph Harper
Linkedin: Ralph Harper

CHAPTER TWELVE

Moving from Death to Life

Sharise Rochelle Quarrles

L iving in darkness, I was blind to how I treated myself and others. I didn't realize how my decisions affected those around me. My long-term relationships had always been physically or mentally abusive, and often both. My fiancé, the father of our three children, beat me until I was almost deaf, and pointed a gun at my head while I begged for my life.

When I was in the hospital after another terrible beating, his probation officer said something that finally stuck with me: *He could have killed you.* At that moment I realized I had to think about my children and fight for my family.

When I pressed charges against my fiancé, it was his third strike, and his conviction led to a 10-year prison sentence. That also meant there'd be no financial support; I was on my own.

Though it was a struggle to be a single mother, I can honestly say God always provided. I didn't feel alone; I felt loved because God saved my life and gave me another chance for life. I also had help from my loving parents who I could never repay.

Although I had been bitter, I have since learned to be better and forgive instead.

I had lots to be bitter about when it came to my relationships with the people who supposedly loved me. My never-ending cycle of pain began when I was a young child and my grandfather raped me. I could never forgive, I carried hate in my heart that made me bitter and unable to move forward. Years later, when I tried to imagine what caused him to become a preacher, a police officer, and a rapist, all at the same time, I was finally able to let it go and forgive him.

My experience with my grandfather also made me view authority in an ungodly way, especially police and preachers. I eventually learned there are some good and bad types everywhere and learned to respect authority.

The Choice

This day I call heaven and earth as witnesses against you that I have set before your life and death, blessings, and curses. Now choose life, so that you and your children may live . . . —

I chose life. I chose life and Jesus. I chose to forgive, love, to be kind, and to love my enemies—though I'm still working on this last part. I wanted to think better thoughts and never fall into a cycle of broken, toxic friendships and relationships again. When God helps us through our battles in life, there is something to learn. If we don't realize or recognize the lesson, we can find ourselves on repeat, as I did, with the lesson presenting itself in several different ways.

We know God is trying to instill in us what we need so we can live our lives and win our battles, but we miss His clues. Every day we need to ask ourselves, *What message is God sending?*

Is it patience I need? Should I be waiting instead of rushing?

Is He teaching me humility? He shines His light equally on the just and unjust, so should I see the people around me from a different perspective, through new eyes, before I condemn another?

Is it more faith that I need? Without it, it's impossible to please God. I have listened to the voice of God and trusted Him through my entire life. I have been to the altar more than seven times to dedicate and rededicate my life to Christ. This is my testimony.

The year 2019 was a time of miracles in the church I attend, and that year built my faith, step by step.

In the first week of January 2019, one of my older daughters called me. She's been battling mental illness, both bipolar disorder, and schizophrenia, and she was having trouble. We spoke, and then I drove to work. Right after I clocked in at the school where I teach, I heard God tell me, *She needs you to come out there now—your grandson needs you.* I battled in my mind for a second, but then I went to my boss. She said, "Yes, you can leave, but I'd appreciate it if you could wait a while and leave later today."

I said, "I need to go **NOW**, it's an hour-and-a half-drive." Another teacher took over my classroom for what I thought would be one day. It became months, and I had to get an unpaid medical leave of absence. I had to choose my family over my job, and I would do it again without hesitating.

My family kept asking me, "Why? You need the money."

I just couldn't imagine letting my five-year-old grandson go back into the child protective services system for the third time since he was an infant. His birthday is January 12, and my daughter had been hospitalized on his birthday for three years in a row.

Events have patterns, and I prayed against them, trying to cancel the devil's plans for my family on the important dates we celebrated. I asked God to take authority over the evil that was trying to take us over. I am proud to say that in 2020, my daughter spent her son's birthday with him. We saw evil creep in, making her have temper tantrums, but we recognized it and prayed it out. I said, "The devil doesn't want you to be out for your son's birthday, but you will be out in Jesus' name."

Speak truly of life no matter how it looks.

Continuing with the year 2019 and the faith builders I experienced, that was the year when a granddaughter was born. Soon after, I had to officially take custody of my granddaughter and grandson. On the way home from the courthouse with my newborn granddaughter, I missed an exit and slid off the road facing the wrong way. I prayed as I saw the oncoming traffic, and just then a huge truck pulled over to help us.

I drove away with some damage to the door and no side-view mirror, but with not a scratch on me or my granddaughter. Once again, I felt like I had a new lease on life and I gave my thanks and praise to the Lord.

I *am* truly thankful and I love to praise the name of the Lord; He has saved me and my family! I still pray for our salvation, and he is saving my children one at a time. I'm thankful to say my daughter is living for God and currently working on getting her children back.

After that, I thought I was up to my full capacity in faith, but then it was tested two more times and elevated me to places I never knew I could be. I lost my job twice; once because I had to care for my grandson, and after being taken back, a second time because of caring for my granddaughter. I applied for a couple of positions for which I didn't feel I qualified, but God told me to apply and I obeyed. I was hired at both places, and I'm still working for one of them. That experience boosted my confidence in Christ and made me see my worth. When God takes away your little teddy (your plans, your attitude, your fears, your ego, that man or woman who wasn't sent by God, those friends and perhaps even family, *your* agenda), He has something greater ahead for you—*His* plan!

Right before Thanksgiving, my bedridden dad suffered a heart attack that left him in the Intensive Care Unit for more than a month. I am grateful my father made it to 2020, thanks only to God's grace.

Remember, in Christ Jesus, you have the victory! Don't be intimidated by your time of trouble; it, too, shall pass. *Do not fear, never give up! Jesus loves you!* Focus on your God, not your problems.

I pray God will continue to protect you and your family, and I pray you break every chain with which the enemy tries to bind you. Suited up with God's full armor, you are protected.

Finally, be strong in the Lord and in His mighty power. Put on the full armor of God, so that you can take your stand against the devil's schemes. For our struggle is not against flesh and blood, but against the rulers, against the authorities, against the powers of this dark world and against the spiritual forces of evil in the heavenly realms. Therefore put on the full armor of God, so that when the day of evil comes, you may be able to stand your ground, and after you have done everything, to stand. Stand firm then, with the belt of truth buckled around your waist, with the breastplate of righteousness in place, and with your feet fitted with the readiness that comes from the gospel of peace. In addition to all this, take up the shield of faith, with which you can extinguish all the flaming arrows of the evil one. Take the helmet of salvation and the sword of the Spirit, which is the word of God. And pray in the Spirit on all occasions with all kinds of prayers and requests. With this in mind, be alert and always keep on praying for all the Lord's people.—**Ephesians 6:10-18 (New International Version)**

Intercede! Be the one to speak life over you, your family, your community, and God's people.

When I look back at all that my family and I have been through over the years, I am astonished at the suffering. My aunt lost her child early in life, and her response was to share and spread her pain. She prayed that I would die—her own sister's child! For years, she told me that—praying for negativity for my family.

My parents' loving marriage was destroyed, and three generations of our family's children were taken from their parents' homes—my mom's, mine, and my daughter's. My daughter's father was addicted to drugs, and once sold her for a fix.

I look at this generational curse, and I say *no more* in Jesus' name! I am free, my family is free, in Jesus' name. AMEN! To see my children suffer in poverty, I say *no more* in Jesus' Name! To see my children going to the hospital more than 20 times, in and out of mental institutions—*no more in Jesus' name!*

Jehovah Rapha (God the healer) has healed my father, my daughter, and my mother's diabetes in Jesus' name. We are healed emotionally, spiritually, financially, mentally—in *all* ways—and we will be *whole*, with nothing missing, nothing lacking, nothing broken in Jesus' name. Abundance is ours. We will live a *full* life in God

My father was healing from his heart attacks much faster than was expected, and then he suddenly passed just before the coronavirus outbreak. His passing brought me an unusual peace, a comfort that he's in a better place with our heavenly father, and it helped me face another fear of mine—death. I am now at peace with death.

Remember no matter what you go through, you are *not* what you survived. You are the *victor*, not the victim!

I thank God for my long period of suffering. He allowed me to be humble so He could do His good work in me and my family and for anyone who believes! I stand only because of God. I give Him my life as I pray for my family's salvation. I have hope despite it all. I know in my weakness that Jesus is my strength.

It's 2:40 a.m., and as I talk with God, He has me think about what I've been through, what I've learned, and then He has me pray for my enemies. He tells me to have compassion for those who wish death upon me, which is something I know I can't do with just my own strength. As I pray that God's will be done for them and myself, I cry, and I know I must give God glory, praise Him, and love Him!

No matter what you have been through or what you may be going through, *have hope*! Know God has never left you; put your faith in God.

I know my life is a life of faith. My life puts faith over fear, and I *never give up*! Jesus motivates me more than the amazing leaders I hear, my family, or anything I can imagine. He made me remember I am loved even when I didn't love myself.

Above all else, love is the key.

For all those years, I was looked down upon, and I believed it was my due, being in abusive ungodly relationships as if that's all I was worth. Once Jesus' love shined into me and helped me see my infirmities and to repent all I have done wrong, the hurt I caused others was removed as I made sincere apologies. I was able to move forward.

Once you are in a true relationship with God and put the time into giving Him the glory despite your circumstances, you can get through anything. You can do all things through Christ because He gives you strength.

You don't have to remember my name or my story, but if you don't remember anything else from this chapter, just remember *Jesus.* Build your personal relationship with Him, trust Him, and have faith in Him, no matter what! He can work miracles and bring you through it all.

I'm just an ordinary person loved by an extraordinary God. I failed over and over again, and it's not that I haven't had my own set of problems. All my problems haven't disappeared since I gave my life to Jesus, yet I now know the peace that passes all my understanding. I went from being a curse maker to a curse breaker, with salvation assurance, on the winning side.

This is my testimony.

If you are going through something, *keep going* (John 14:27)! You're in good company. Joseph, Moses, Joshua, and other biblical people of faith suffered greatly as they built *great faith.* On the other side of your suffering, challenges, and adversity, is VICTORY!

For everyone reading my testimony, I pray that you break through and have continuous breakthroughs until your enemies are overthrown. Walk in obedience to King Jesus and finish your race. I pray that we hear *well done* and that we mature into who He wants by repenting daily, asking for help from our Father in Heaven, and allowing ourselves to receive His best.

Your character is being molded through your situation, building you and perfecting you to carry out the work that God has called and chosen you to complete. Find the secret place of the most high by building a personal intimate relationship with Him. Know and understand Jesus.

I pray we experience the abundant life God has planned! Abundant in peace, love, blessings, healing, deliverance, salvation, and all the good things God has for you when you do not faint. Grow in wisdom and understanding, and I pray we will continue to believe throughout all we face.

Know you are covered by the blood of Jesus.

YOU SHALL LIVE.

YOU SHALL NOT DIE.

YOU are BLESSED.

Allow God to rearrange what He wants in your life and to take what He wants so you will grow into His plan, not the expectations you or others have. He has plans to help you prosper, to bless you, for all things are working for your good.

It may not be what you want now, but believe that when you let go of that little teddy to receive the bigger and better teddy, believe that you will receive much better. Submit to God so you can receive what He has written in the Book of Life for you and your generations. Be blessed and leave a legacy of obedience, love, worship, and faith in the Lord Jesus Christ. AMEN.

It is so worth it! Your present pain cannot compare to God's glory, building that relationship with God, meditating on His word, and dwelling in His secret place.

I pray that suicide is stopped, that abortions will end, mothers and fathers will rethink their options, racist acts across our globe will cease, our rights as God's children be handed back to us, that we walk in our God-given authority, that families be whole and healed, single parents find the means to provide and thrive, marriages be restored and the divorce rate will be lowered, that faith keeps growing, souls keep being saved, and that we find the narrow road and travel like never before because we know who and whose we are and we have the confidence in Christ Jesus. May we be successful letting go of the heavy burdens and putting on the light yoke, and finish the race we started, going back to our first love, Jesus. In Jesus' name, I pray, Amen!

The most important and greatest lesson is to *love!* God loves us! In order to be useful, we need to allow God to correct us so even when you're going through the beating, pressing, and pruning, keep going. It may not feel good, but keep going, *just keep going.* You will make it if you ask God for His strength and don't grow weary. You will complete the race in Jesus' name. Amen.

For if you live according to the flesh you will die, but if by the Spirit you put to death the misdeeds of the body, you will live.
Romans 8:13 (NIV)

Biography

Sharise was born in Tacoma, Washington, one of Juliette and Michael Anthony's five children. After earning a full scholarship to Newbury College in Brookline, Massachusetts, she graduated from Roxbury Community College with a degree in Business Management. She's also attended classes at the University of Massachusetts for drug counseling, Gordon Theology, MASSArt for fashion, and Urban College for teaching. She works at Leading Edge, where she's a Site coordinator.

A single mother of four adult children and one pre-teenager, she currently lives in Boston, Massachusetts, with her children and two grandchildren. They attend Jubilee Boston Church.

Contact Information

Email: sharisequarrles@gmail.com
Website: shariserochellequarrles.org
Instagram: shariseq81
Facebook: Sharise Quarrles
LinkedIn: Sharise Quarrles
YouTube: Sharise

CHAPTER THIRTEEN

Get Up! AGAIN!

Toni L. Pennington

Half of surviving is attitude. Unfortunately, it took years before I managed to grasp that concept.

When I had three surgeries for fibroids, I didn't get it. When I thought I was dying and had blood clots in my lungs, I couldn't believe it. And when my test came back positive for HIV, I was completely devastated.

That day I believed my life was over.

My dream of sharing my life with a true partner now seemed impossible. I would never get married. I mourned. I had a bleak vision of growing old, all alone, eating dinner at a long table with a cat sitting on the other end, and it terrified me.

My medical problems started off dramatically, with fibroids "growing like wildfire," as my gynecologist so graphically described them. I was extremely anemic. Sometimes I felt like I was dying. I could barely climb a flight of stairs. I was often afraid that I couldn't make it from one place to the next without bleeding through my clothes. I was embarrassed. Now I realize how ridiculous that thinking was. Why would I be embarrassed for being sick? Surgery was the only option.

Five years later, I was in the same situation. My previous doctor had retired and my new doctor was wonderful. He believed in minimally invasive procedures, but, he was forced to open me up, as had the first doctor. The third time, a sonogram revealed the scarring from previous surgeries and the new fibroids made it impossible to save my uterus. It had to go.

While I'd never yearned for children, once that possibility was taken from me, I felt a loss. I still wasn't married and I had no idea whether someone might come into my life whom I could imagine as the father of our children. But it was what it was. I had the surgery.

When I got past that hurdle, another one was right around the corner. I was lying in bed watching television when I felt like a dagger was ripping my heart out of my chest.

The pain got worse. I'd never felt anything like it. Was I having a heart attack? The shock bolted me into an upright position. It was as if someone snatched the front of my pajama top and sat me up like a puppet. I was stunned. The thump of my heartbeat pounded in my eardrums.

I was afraid, but I couldn't call anyone. I knew they would insist that I go to the hospital and I did not want to go. I settled back against a pile of pillows, afraid to lie prone, praying that I would wake up in the morning. I figured if I died my neighbors would smell my rotting corpse and eventually the cops would break the door down, or my brother or sister would investigate if they couldn't reach me.

My behavior that night was incredibly stupid, but that's what I did.

The following day I went to work as usual. The scare of the previous night crossed my mind, but I ignored it. In the weeks to come, I continued my routines –work, school, rehearsals. I was determined to be who I was before I'd ever been ill, an active, healthy woman.

After six months I was losing my ability to breathe. My decline was slow. I was so busy, I really didn't notice what was happening to my body.

One cold night, I was leaving to go to class. Even though I hate socks and almost never wear them, I was afraid I'd be cold so I grabbed a pair. I sat on the side of the bed to put them on. When I bent over, I lost my breath. Tears welled up in my eyes.

Intuitively, I knew something was seriously wrong with my body. I could no longer deny it. I called a friend and asked her to take me to the hospital.

Both my mother and father died due to heart issues, and I was afraid it was my heart. I had already outlived my mother's short life of 39 years, so I was relieved when I heard the emergency room nurse say, "Pennington's been rejected from cardiac care." I had blood clots in my lungs.

I would never have imagined that my issue would be my lungs. After all, I was a singer. I walked, I danced, I didn't smoke. I didn't do any of the things that I thought could impair them. My visit turned into six days in intensive care and four additional days of the medical staff trying to find the right combination of blood thinners.

After I was released and went for my follow-up appointment, my doctor asked if a student could sit in on my appointment. Always the comedian, I replied, "Of course, I'm interesting." Dr. C. chuckled and the student entered the room.

"Patient was diagnosed with a spray of blood clots in her lungs."

"Wait . . . what? A *spray*? I thought I had like two or three in each one."

"No. You had sprays of blood clots in both your lungs."

I swore I had never heard this. It turned out that a clot had pinched off because of the fibroids and traveled up into my lungs and disseminated. I was one of 13 known cases like that ever. Once my doctor explained the rarity of my case, I asked him if we were going to make any money or at least be featured in JAMA (Journal of American Medical Association).

Sadly, he said no. Oh well. For six months, I had been a walking time bomb. I could have dropped dead in the street.

After the clot episode, I was instructed to go directly to an emergency room if I ever felt anything strange in my chest. Later that same year when I had chest pains, I went straight to the hospital. Tests showed my white blood cell count was unusually high, suggesting my body was trying to fight something really aggressive. When they asked if they could test me for HIV, I said "Of course." I had been tested before and the results had always been negative. I wasn't worried.

Three months passed before I got the results. That day Dr. G told me my viral load was 1,280,000 and my T cells were at 198. Anything less than 200 is considered AIDS.

My immediate thought was that I couldn't tell my brother or sister. This news would destroy them. I went out to my car and sat for a while. I knew, besides living the rest of my life alone, I would never laugh again. That really hurt. I decided that I needed to tell the person I was seeing at the time immediately because I didn't think I would have the nerve if any time passed. I drove directly to his job praying the whole time that I would be focused and not get into a car accident. He wasn't there. Then God blessed me.

As I drove home and stopped at a red light, I heard yelling. I looked around and saw a very small man on a very large motorcycle. The man had his arms stretched up in the air holding onto his super-high ape-hanger handlebars, his cell phone was tucked into a cap under his helmet, and he was yelling into the phone.

So much for my lifetime without laughter. I started laughing, and I laughed for at least five minutes. When I stopped, I thanked God for answering me immediately. I felt as though He said, "I know you just heard something that will change your life forever, but it's not going to be the way you think."

I hadn't lost my sense of humor because I had gotten bad news. Funny things were still going to happen, and I was still going to laugh.

All this is to say, no matter how dark the days may be, embrace the small things that bring you joy. They are small and they are personal. Your pleasures may not be like anyone else's, but if they make you happy, embrace them.

I went home, got in bed and cried. I cried and I cried. I thought about people I knew who were mean, hateful, nasty and downright unkind. Most were married and seemed to have great lives. Why was this happening to *me*? What great sin had *I* committed? I blamed myself. AIDS was the number-one thing I was afraid of and here I was—dying. Not only with a positive diagnosis but with a stratospheric viral load.

But God was still communicating with me.

After I wrapped my mind around my reality, I came back to myself. I recognized that this awful disease was not representative of who I was. It did not wipe away 45 years of life. Everything I had accomplished to that point did not disappear. *I was still me.*

I made the decision to choose life. That day, my doctor gave me a prescription for the medication that I still take today. Within 30 days my viral load dropped to 1800 and my T cells increased to 213. I was not dying.

I have shared my story because I want people to understand that you can choose life.

After three surgeries to remove fibroids and eventually my uterus, I chose life.

After a 10-day stay in the hospital due to pulmonary emboli, I chose life.

After my devastating HIV diagnosis, I chose life.

I knew I had more life to live. I certainly had more to give. There was still a whole world I wanted to see. It may sound as if I'm over-simplifying health issues. I am not. All of my issues have been extremely serious, and two were life-threatening, but I believe that God's plan was to use me.

I thought back to the 1980s when I lost friends to AIDS. When I visited one of them I saw maybe a dozen vials of medication on the table. I peeked at one and the label said Azidothymidine (AZT), which I knew was the drug used to fight AIDS. My friend took over 30 pills every day. They did not save his life. 25 years later I am allowed to live. I take one pill a day.

I don't ask why. I only say thank you. My beloved reminds me occasionally that I am a walking miracle. Sometimes I forget (he'll love reading this).

Half the battle of dealing with life's grief and pain is attitude. You've got to look up. There's nothing below you but the ground—dirt, or worse, cement. Above you is the sky and all possibilities.

Three days after the HIV diagnosis, I went for a previously scheduled biopsy on my thyroid. That was the same day the New York Giants were being celebrated with a parade along the Canyon of Heroes in downtown Manhattan. I told the doctor that my HIV test had come back positive. I could see that he was surprised by my calm demeanor. He asked me to repeat it. I did.

"When did you find this out?" he asked.

"Two days ago."

He stared at me for a few seconds then he covered my hand with his, smiled and said, "You're going to be all right. You know why?"

I shook my head, about to cry.

"Your attitude. Half of surviving these kinds of things is attitude. I'm not going to do the biopsy. Good luck to you."

I threw my hands up and said, "Okay, then I'm goin' to the parade!"

"I wish I could," he said.

We laughed and he disappeared behind the curtain. I got dressed and left. I walked to the train station, squeezed into a sea of blue, surrounding myself with happiness. In spite of what I was dealing with, being at the parade was the best medicine. That day was such a blessing. It was greater than happiness. I was surrounded by pure joy. For a few hours that joy seeped into my soul. It was the beginning of my healing.

Don't get me wrong. I'm not saying that I didn't regress. Remember, the two previous days were spent in tears, bitter tears. I don't remember eating, going to the bathroom—all I remember is tears. But I got up. That was more than a decade ago.

As long as you get up you can win. Always get up. Put one foot in front of the other and begin to move forward.

How do you move forward when you feel defeated? The simple answer is that you push. You push through. I would never suggest that pushing is easy. It is not. If there is anyone on this planet that you love—a sister, brother, parents, a spouse, children, a pet; use them as your guiding light. Push toward them. Let love support you.

Personally, I believed God always told me when to share my story with someone. I shared it one person at a time. Usually, someone chose to confide in me about an extreme trial that they were facing. I did not use my illness to say, "Oh you think that's something? Get a load of this!" Absolutely not! I prayed that sharing my experiences would offer hope.

For people who know me very well, there's probably been no time when they haven't seen me being creative, joking, vibrant and enjoying life. That's how people see Toni Pennington. My fear of sinking into an abyss of depression and mental and emotional paralysis was greater than attempting to make it through another day so I pushed and am still pushing.

My story is not the worst thing that ever happened to anyone, but I've had people say, "Oh, I don't know what I would do."

My answer has always been and will always be, "You'd do what I did. You would ask the doctors and you'd ask God or whoever or whatever you believe in, "What do I do next?" And you'd be here telling me your story. Believe me. I lived it." Some chuckle. Some simply nod as if to say, "I get it." And in that moment I feel that my work is done.

Today, my viral load remains undetectable and my T cells are well above 1000. I am alive. I am happy. I am in love. And I enjoy every day that God gives me.

Biography

Toni Pennington is a Brooklyn, New York native currently living in Jersey City, New Jersey. She holds a Bachelor of Arts degree in English from New Jersey City University.

Although she has been a singer for most of her life, she has found great joy in writing. Toni enjoys her job as an Academic Success Coach and Tutor Mentor at NJCU. She has hosted and participated in several Student Symposiums. She is published in several issues of *PATHS*, one of the school's literary volumes, and is currently working on her Master of Arts degree at Southern New Hampshire University.

Contact Information:

Email: joyforeverenterprises@gmail.com
Website: joyforeverenterprises.com
Instagram: Joyforever1love
Twitter: Joyforever108

CHAPTER FOURTEEN

We Are Unstoppable

Reagan Jasmin

Where I lived, in a depressed, crime-ridden area of South Africa, it was rare to be born into a family in which your mother and father were married to each other. It did not seem like a blessing when I was very young, though, because my father was in the military and stationed away from home most of the time.

After he left the military, my father was unemployed for years and my mother was the sole wage earner. She would return home from her retail job exhausted and frustrated, still finding time and money to bring home a small piece of chocolate candy for me. I was just a child but I could sense the financial pressure weighing heavy on my mother.

Her feet were constantly sore from work and all the walking she had to do—a common complaint among those who lived in our racially mixed neighborhood during the apartheid era in South Africa. I was too young to really experience apartheid, but I did have a taste of it.

Where we lived during the 1980s was infested with gangsterism and drugs. It calmed down during the 1990s and then the violence rose again. Crime flourishes whenever unemployment is high.

When I was six, my parents sent me to live with my mother's family because they believed it would be safer there. My Granny's home in Newlands East was a very Christian environment, with gospel music always playing in the background. The music I heard spoke to me, and it was the foundation for my Christianity. For the first eight years of my life, things seemed to be going well with our family. We did not have much, but it was all I knew.

After my father found a job, my parents moved into their own house in Newlands East. Their work kept them both away from home for 12 hours at a time, so I still spent most of my time with Granny. She was my pillar of strength and the one who raised me.

When I started living with my parents again, my father took his frustrations out on me. He seemed to have two personalities. At times, he was a good person and father. At other times, he had a mean side. Being around him felt like walking on eggs because I never knew which version of him would show up.

When I was twelve, I began seeing more of his mean side. I thought his anger was my fault. If I commented, I was wrong. If I kept quiet and looked away, then I was challenging him. My foundation always had been church, but even that was an issue for my father. It was confusing and stressful. I started to fear him and I was angry. All I wanted to do was to finish school so that I could leave home.

I used to believe my mother was not doing enough to protect me and that angered me more. I needed an outlet and had none. Abusers control the people around them and what they do, and my father was no exception.

I experimented with marijuana because I knew he would be angry if he found out. Marijuana was my escape and rebellion.

Just before my dad would arrive home from work each day, I headed out to smoke with my friends, knowing he would smell it on me when I came home. I eventually moved to harder drugs. I knew he would be angry if he knew I was taking them and that gave me satisfaction. I took drugs to hurt him, not to hurt myself.

One day my parents and I had a massive disagreement and I left home. I was determined to make my parents feel the same pain I felt.

Initially, I moved back to my grandmother's home—my place of refuge—but I left because my parents would know where to find me. I did not know where I was going; I just wanted to get out of their lives.

At the time, I had a weekend job. After work, I walked the streets of Durban all night and then would head back to that job exhausted. One night while wandering, I bumped into a friend of mine, Anthony (Ants) who asked where I was staying. I told him I had no place to stay.

"What do you mean that you have no place to stay?" Ants said. "You can stay at my house, bro."

For several months, I lived at his parents' home. During that time, we were always high, skipping school, and heading down a highway of destruction. But I knew I wanted more out of life.

I was adamant that I was finished with my parents and did not want to see them.

There was a community park where my friends and I used to hang out. Every Friday, my father would finish work at about noon and would drive past. I noticed him, but paid no attention. One Friday, he did not drive past. I figured he must have been working late.

At 3 p.m. that day, I was standing outside my friend's house and my mother and other family members pulled up and asked to talk to me. I got in the car.

"Daddy has passed away," my mother told me and she burst into tears.

I was silent, I did not know what to say or how to feel.

"Why would you lie like that?" I finally asked, confused and a little afraid. "If you want me to come home, just tell me." I could not believe he was dead because he had never been ill. It made no sense.

I went home with my mother and learned she had been telling the truth.

I felt guilty and wondered if my actions had been worth it. All I could remember were the good things about him and regret consumed me. I blamed myself. I thought maybe if I had been a better son instead of being so rebellious, he would be alive. I felt as if I was being buried under layers of negativity.

Eventually I learned that before he died, my father asked my mother for help. "Pray for me," he asked humbly. "I want to give my life to God."

Mother did pray for him. Three days later he passed away. Many people do not have the opportunity to make a breakthrough like that before they die.

After he passed, I looked for every reason to take responsibility for his death. The pain of the loss and the regret was slowly starting to break me down.

When we discovered his death was caused by being poisoned, I wanted to hurt the responsible person. The emotions I was feeling—loss, guilt, anger—were wrecking my brain and my heart. I started hearing stories of how my father had asked about me daily, which shocked me. I had thought he did not care. Could it be he just did not know how to treat me?

Later I learned people who have been hurt tend to hurt other people, and I believe that was the case between my father and me. My father was doing what he knew. Hurting people can be a vicious cycle, but I finally broke it through forgiveness.

My father's brother and I are very close, and he always treated me with love and respect. I could not understand why two brothers were so different despite growing up in the same environment. But both men made different decisions—one allowed their past to make them into a better person and one allowed the past to change them into an angry stranger. Understanding that helped me realize I did not have to fall victim to the way I had been treated; I could be better than that.

My mother's brother-in-law decided I needed a break from everything that was going on, and he said I should visit him in Johannesburg. This uncle always treated me as if I was his own son and I believed he was the type of father I deserved.

My uncle offered guidance, built me up, motivated me, and was a pillar of strength. He trusted me no matter what anyone said. He also believed my father wanted the best for me even though I could not yet see it.

In my uncle's home, I had access to lots of personal development material which played a major role in my personal breakthrough. Those simple yet profound books contained stories that changed my perspective on life.

I focused on God's word. I attended church, and paid close attention to every sermon. I began to feel the preacher talked directly to me, and it lit a fire within me. I started believing I could motivate people. I realized I am a man who can impact people's lives with a story most people *go through* and but many do not know how to *grow through*.

During this period, I learned the power of speaking things into existence, visualization, and the power of the subconscious mind by immersing myself in motivating materials.

I began to realize my father taught me some valuable lessons. I knew that if it was not for him, I would not have been able to handle some of life's challenges.

My father's words often pierced me deeply, but now I know I am the opposite of everything negative he called me.

But my challenges and pain did not end with my father's death.

Two years after my father's passing, I was back visiting relatives in Durban when I bumped into an old friend, Dallin Godfrey, who could relate to me because his dad also had passed away. We were always close, and we were together daily during my visit.

After I was back in Johannesburg, Dallin called and asked me to be his best man for his wedding and to come to his engagement party. The day I arrived, he had an argument with his fiancée and left their apartment without saying anything to me, which was unlike him.

I went looking for Dallin, could not find him, and returned to their apartment to sleep. I woke at midnight and heard his fiancée crying because she was concerned about him. In the morning, we received a call that a body had been found at a nearby school and it might be him.

When I was approximately 300 feet from his body, I knew it was my friend. Anger and shock took over and all I wanted was revenge.

"I should have been with him and maybe he would be alive or maybe we would both be dead, but we would have been together," I thought.

We buried Dallin on the day that had been scheduled for his engagement party. At the funeral, his family reacted oddly toward me, and I learned they believed I had murdered my best friend. I had no clue why, but I did understand people usually need someone to blame.

Dealing with the loss and being accused of murder had me questioning myself again. People asked why, when we always had been together, was I not there—or maybe I had been?—when he needed me most.

I did not have the energy to respond to their accusations.

While the investigation was going on, I stayed in Durban with my aunt and uncle. It was lonely and traumatizing. The murder was eating away at me.

My uncle came home one day and told me I had to leave. I remember walking the streets alone late at night asking, "God, why this is happening? What is the lesson? How can there be a lesson in this?"

I had walked the same routes before, but Dallin always had been with me. Sometimes you must walk alone on a painful path and that is when God will reveal his plan to you. However, if someone had told me that at that moment, I would have thought it was a joke.

I forgave those who accused me and the person who killed my friend. I was at peace and God had my attention and I realized I had no control over what transpired. I could not have saved my friend or prevented his death.

When I was called to the police to identify some items that were stolen from Dallin, I learned the murderer, a male acquaintance of ours, had been apprehended. I was relieved; I had already forgiven him.

Withholding forgiveness will consume you and delay your

breakthrough. During the investigation and trial, I discovered a strength within myself I never knew existed. I learned how the power of decision and the power of forgiveness can heal any person.

Simply forgive.

When we utilize that deeper power inside us all, we are *unstoppable.* Our test becomes our testimony.

I survived this experience knowing bad things may still happen to me and those I love. Yet now I know I am a conqueror, a child of God, and everything that happens to me builds me up into a stronger force that cannot be destroyed.

You can run from adversity or learn from it; if you do not learn, you will be trapped in an endless recycling of the trouble. Tell yourself you can get through whatever it is. Surround yourself with people who believe in you and material that inspires you.

It worked for me and it will work for you.

God's plan is for you to prosper in your life. Sometimes you must overcome adversity to fulfill God's plan and your purpose. Sometimes it is unfair and unreasonable, but these challenges can be the foundation for personal breakthrough.

If you look deep enough, you can find the lesson in every situation. What may seem like a *setback* is a *set-up* for God to bless you.

Your breakthrough is waiting for you and you have a choice: Are you going to receive it? I made that choice. I chose to break the cycle of pain and unforgiveness and build a family bond that is unbreakable.

Biography

Reagan Keith Jasmin is an entrepreneur, international motivational speaker and experienced protection specialist who was brought up in an underprivileged neighborhood in South Africa.

His breakthrough came at a young age while he served as a private military contractor in Iraq. The experience altered his perspective and brought out the purpose of his life, which is to inspire people young and old. Today, he has made it his life's mission to improve peoples' lives by being an example that you can achieve anything in life if you put your mind to it, no matter how tough the circumstances.

Contact Information:

For more information, contact Reagan at:
reaganjasmin@gmail.com
Facebook: Reagan Keith Jasmin
Instagram: breakthruwit_reags
Twitter: breakthruwit_reags

CHAPTER FIFTEEN

Rising from the Ashes

Carol Gockel

She Fell

She fell
She crashed
She broke
She cried
She crawled
She hurt
She surrendered
And then . . .
She rose again

—Nausicaa Twila *(Used with permission from the author.)*

The room was dark. I could not tell where I was. I turned my head to the right to open my left eye to get a wider view of my surroundings only to find my eye glued shut. As I pulled my body to turn toward my right, a sharp pain in the back of my neck caused me to bury my face in the pillow once again.

The left side of my body felt numb, I could not feel my arm. I turned slowly onto my back and realized I was naked. Disoriented,

I tried to search the room for some indication of where I was. My fingers felt the linen underneath, a familiar sensation; the air was warm and the scent stale. The ceiling fan was rotating silently above as my mind started to understand: I am on my mattress, I am in my room, and I am still alive.

Tears started streaming from the corners of my eyes once more, uncontrollably like the many times before. My throat, dry and sore, could barely make a whimper. Then came the tsunami of pain pouring out of every inch of my body like hundreds of spikes piercing through my skin at once. I howled in agony as I felt ripped apart from the inside, clenching my fists tightly on my sheets.

Curling myself into a fetal position, I soundlessly wailed in the sparsely furnished room and surrendered to my demise; humiliated, ashamed, discarded, $100,000 in debt, penniless, alone in an apartment for which I could not afford the rent. Feeling worthless, stupid, and used I mourned for the loss of my identity, my life, and a decade of my youth.

ⵗ ⵗ ⵗ

I was juggling school with part-time work to make extra pocket money. He was a student at the university where I was working at the bazaar that day. Halfway through my sales pitch at the booth, he gave me his number, invited me to call that evening to speak further, and then rushed off to his lecture.

The boss decided to take us out to celebrate at the hottest club in town for our work that weekend. Eager to close one more sale, I called him to arrange to meet at the club.

He appeared out of nowhere and handed me a glass of Long Island Iced Tea. We chatted. Before I knew it, the entire group of people I had arrived with had left me behind. He offered to drive me home.

I have wondered how my life would have been had I not

accepted that ride home.

Ever since I was a young girl, it had been instilled in me that girls grew up to be married off and become a member of her husband's family. I would bear their name, have children to honor the family, and be cherished by a loving husband for my entire life.

My brothers and I went to a neighborhood school; I was an average student, not particularly bright. My parents' expectations were only that we would score high enough to move on to the next grade. They never pressured us to excel. Life was living from paycheck to paycheck, going through the motions every day—just "being." My father told me to take care of my looks and to stay attractive enough to "marry up" so I would not have to work my buttocks off—to meet someone who would provide for me.

That shaped my idea of what my life role should be: a domestic goddess, loving mother to my brood, living in a nice house, with a husband who'd support us financially. I had a list of criteria for my would-be spouse. He would be:

- attractive, but not overly so,
- successful, or on track to be,
- charismatic,
- devoted to me, and
- dedicated to loving and caring for me forever

And there he was, sitting next to me in the car as he drove me home. He bought the car himself with money he made as a real estate agent while juggling school as a student. He shared his desire to be self-reliant and not ask his father for money. He was a rugby star, yet he exuded a quiet confidence, almost mysterious. He wasn't showy like the boys I'd met from privileged backgrounds.

Before I got out of the car, he asked if he could call to get to know me better. I thought, "He is different. He wants to get to know me for *me*."

I took the bait.

I'm from what's considered a working-class Singapore family. My mother left school at a young age to help look after her siblings while my maternal grandparents, immigrants from China, toiled hard as manual laborers.

My father came from a middle-class upbringing. He was the youngest of five children, and after high school he went to work in the grocery store my grandfather owned. After my parents married and bought a flat, my mother was a stay-at-home parent raising three children. My dad worked in the entertainment industry, starting his shifts at night, and returning during the day to sleep.

My background could not have been more different from his. Based on our academic achievements, upbringing, and circle of friends, we would never have met were it not for that day at the bazaar. Within months of our meeting, I moved in with him.

Living together is frowned upon in Asian culture—it's a disgrace to the family. But I was head over heels in love with him, and I could not have cared less what others thought of me, not even my parents.

There were only a handful of explosive outbursts during our relationship: throwing a wine glass on the floor, kicking the furniture, breaking a mirror. There was nothing overtly physical toward me that would have made me fear for my safety.

Words were his weapons. It started subtly and innocently—a comment about my clothes, my hair, or my makeup, followed by him scrunching his nose up and shrugging, "Well, it's your choice." He would pass it off as teasing and punctuate his words with a little cheeky laugh.

"That is only expected of you, baby. What you have done is not quite an 'achievement.' I know you can do better," he would tell me in a gentle, yet slightly mocking tone. It was his way of belittling the little triumphs I had worked hard to achieve while disguising his words as encouragement.

I was slowly isolated from my friends because he said they were a bad influence and would hinder my personal growth. I was persuaded to keep my family away, for their working-class status would not go with the image he had carefully created of us.

His cold shoulders, silent treatment, and withholding of affection ebbed away the foundation of my being. He began to often twist his words to deny promises he'd made or words he'd said in the past. I began to question my own reality and sanity.

His verbal attacks escalated over the years.

Many times, he would give me positive reinforcement only to tear me down, telling me I could be worthy if I just changed my bad personality traits. If anything were to go "wrong" in our relationship, he told me, it would be because I had not heeded his advice or sought his approval before acting.

That was how he exerted control over me. His look of contempt, disgust, sadness, and disappointment combined with his voice and tone always made me feel terrible. I was chided until I conformed to his wishes.

There was no shouting from his end, only from mine. I had to defend myself. My words and my beliefs were begging to be heard. I was angry, frustrated, despondent, and constantly in tears. In his response, he would say in the calmest voice imaginable that I was acting emotionally and irrationally, and if I changed my ways, that would not happen in the future. In a very literal sense, I was a baby for him to mold the way he deemed fit, demeaning me whenever he could and masquerading it as love.

Why didn't I leave? It's hard for those outside our relationship to see the damage within. To outsiders, we were successful and happy. In reality, I was profoundly depressed and had lost whatever self-confidence I'd ever had.

To make it even harder for me to leave, he made sure I was at the mercy of his financial control over my earnings. For the entire thirteen years of our union, he never held a job down for long. He always believed there was a better and faster way to make money, one with minimum input that would yield maximum output.

He invested heavily in high-risk stocks. He eventually declared bankruptcy because of his bad decisions. After going bankrupt, he wasn't allowed to work in the finance sector and he convinced me to start an advertising company.

As the named owner of the company, my paycheck was used to fund the business, pay our employees, and cover living expenses. To appear rich, he had taken on a lifestyle that was too difficult to maintain.

He told me I would have to stay out of the limelight so he could shine. He would constantly berate me for putting on weight, not looking sexy enough, not dressing rich enough, or looking too ordinary. I even had plastic surgery in the hopes that he would approve of me.

I resorted to lying to get higher-paying jobs because he made me, as his wife, responsible for supporting his business endeavors. Living in constant fear of incurring his wrath on the home front, I worked extra hard to ensure my lies on the professional front were not discovered. Business eventually improved, and we were able to secure a loan from the bank where I worked so we could buy an apartment.

My work ethic was what saved me. My confidence grew as I grew professionally and I began to resist his controlling ways.

Throughout the years, he frequently sought attention from other women; finally it was serious enough for him to want to move on. He began to distance himself from me. He exploited my late nights and long hours at work as the reason for our constant bickering. He said he needed to re-evaluate our marriage. I was in a panicked state and I agreed to allow him to move in with a friend to figure things out.

He needed a way to cash out. He concocted an elaborate plan of how he had opened a trading account in my name that accumulated losses of tens of thousands of dollars.

"How about we sell the apartment, close the business down, get cleared of bankruptcy, start afresh, and live a normal life?" he suggested.

As gullible as it seems now, I jumped at the opportunity to be in his favor again. I sold the apartment and took out extra loans to pay off the debts. As soon as the money came into my account, he emptied every single cent and left me with nothing. Then he held the money as a bargaining chip to negotiate for a quick divorce.

For three days I curled up on my mattress with no food or drink. Drifting in and out of consciousness, I wondered why I had not yet died. As the feeling of being destitute pulled me downward in a spiral of despair, I constantly entertained thoughts of death, yet I did not have the courage to hurt myself. I loathed myself for being weak and stupid. It was no wonder he did not want me. If I didn't die of thirst or starvation, I thought, I should be set on fire and burn to death.

My breakthrough came when I heard a voice in my head: *If you die, he wins! He will be enjoying life with his mistress and living on your hard-earned money.* Sorrow turned to anger, and eventually gave me enough strength to lift myself out of bed.

A sharp pain in my stomach sent me to my knees, and I crawled slowly toward the bathroom. The person staring back in the mirror was unrecognizable; her face pale, with burning eyes. I washed up and hobbled my way to the doctor to get treatment for a urinary tract infection.

The psychological abuse suffered over a decade left a lasting imprint on my psyche and emotional well-being. In the years since, I have had to re-learn how to trust and how to communicate effectively with people. I have again learned to let my walls down to let people in. I have learned how to reframe my mind and to love myself first.

Most importantly, I learned to do the hardest thing of all: forgive myself.

I would be lying if I say the journey to self-love and realization was quick and easy. There still are days when I have doubts. Though I'm not diagnosed with Post Traumatic Stress Disorder (PTSD), I did exhibit symptoms associated with it. Certain triggers will give me flashbacks and feelings of inadequacy. Sometimes, uncontrollable thoughts of the painful aftermath pop into my mind, or I feel unmotivated and detached emotionally.

I still cannot recall the entirety of the fateful three days I spent in bed, but I do remember the key pieces of wisdom I gained through surviving the experience and during my recovery:

Have support and help

No one should ever have to go through tough times alone. Create an internal support system from family and friends, and also consider external support in the form of professional help. A professional counselor will give you an outlet in a safe and non-judgmental environment so you can fully process the myriads of emotions and turmoil within you.

Bring Back 'You'

Allow yourself to receive compliments, solicit them, and ask loved ones to tell you what they love about you. Let yourself make mistakes and accept they're all part and parcel of living. Keep a journal to jot down all the things you enjoyed doing in the past. Bring back the *true* you, reclaim the person you are meant to be. And, as cliché as it sounds, a wonderful way to find yourself is to go on a trip or an adventure.

Stop Self-Sabotaging

Be aware of the pitfalls of getting set in a pattern of self-deprecation. Be kind to yourself. Tune out the little critical voice in your head. Embrace the reality: It is perfectly OK to have doubts! Trust that you can always correct the negative thinking by reframing and reassuring yourself that you're worth it and deserve everything good that is coming your way. Be a constant work in progress as you grow to improve daily.

I can't think of anything more appropriate to end my chapter than sharing with you a Chinese saying: *Zhen Jin Bu Pa Huo Lian, meaning true gold fears no fire.*

Gold can be melted into a molten liquid state under extreme heat; however, its properties remain unaltered and it can be re-designed into anything we desire. Our spirits are like gold. We must first be burned and stripped down, then give rise to something beautiful. Like a phoenix, it's rebirth can only come after burning to ashes.

Biography

Carol Gockel is a transformation coach, speaker, and student of life. Her passion for helping people, particularly women, relearn how to love themselves, grew from her breaking through her own personal adversities. She shares her wealth of experience and knowledge on living and creating a fulfilling life with her clients.

Her personal mission is to inspire and empower people to achieve emotional, spiritual, and financial success.

Carol lives in Singapore with her husband and two children, and she loves to cook and explore the world.

Contact Information:

Connect with Carol on social media:
Instagram: www.instagram.com/carolgockel
Facebook: www.facebook.com/carolgockeltransformation
Website: www.CarolGockel.com
Email: carolgockel@gmail.com

CHAPTER SIXTEEN

All About Action

Arturo Lassiter

Someday

One day

Tomorrow

Later

Four words that prevent us from taking immediate action. How many times have you had a task or goal in front of you and thought about putting it off until someday, one day, tomorrow, or later?

The times in my life when I have taken instant, in-the-moment action on a task, goal, or challenge before me are the times when I have experienced the most progress and success.

I knew from an early age that being an employee and working nine-to-five for forty years was not the plan for my life. Living life according to other people's terms and conditions was not something to which I could conform. I was never the model employee and never would be.

Instead, taking action became the important focus of my life, and it defined the dividing line between two very different outcomes in life.

The expectation of others

As a young man, I dreamed of making it big in the music industry. I had a passion and talent for writing and singing, and I had started a singing group in high school. As a group, we were young, talented, and hungry. Our breakout plan for our future boiled down to attending concerts with the hope of meeting and auditioning for major artists.

In 1994, a popular group called *Immature* had a concert in Kansas City. Being a man of action (even back then), I saw opportunity. Though we had no tickets, we drove an hour to Kansas City with full expectations of meeting the group and seeing the concert. After a couple of failed attempts to go backstage, I spoke with a security guard and learned the name of the hotel where band members were staying.

After we waited for hours, the group finally entered the hotel through the front doors and we began our audition—right there in the lobby. The group's manager said he liked our sound and wanted to fly us to Hollywood, California, to work in the studio. Two weeks later, we received plane tickets to Hollywood.

Since I'd been offered a scholarship to college, I had a decision to make—the biggest decision of my life up to that point. It is not easy to pick up and leave what you've known all your life and move halfway across the country with nothing more than a dream.

How many people would set out for a place they have never been, defying all advice and turning down other "realistic" opportunities, in hopes of creating the life you desperately desired? It is all too easy to let the fear of the unknown paralyze your dreams.

My excitement and deep desire to succeed in the music

business was stronger than my fear, so my brother (my music producer) and I packed up and headed to the Golden State; leaving behind college scholarships, friends, family, and everything familiar. I burned my ships, and there was no turning back. Hollywood presented great opportunities as well as great challenges, and I was prepared to tackle them both.

I eventually signed a deal with Universal Records as a song-writer. This was truly a coup, but I was not satisfied. My dream was to be a vocal artist. Being behind the scenes and writing songs for other artists was great, but it wasn't my dream. I made the best of my situation and did well enough to receive a gold album for songs I had written for a popular R&B group.

My gold album was the key that taught me the magic of residual income or royalties. I learned there was another way to make a living that did not require investing tens of thousands of dollars or sacrificing eight to ten hours a day on the hamster wheel: There was a way to do something *one time*, and get paid for that effort residually.

With jobs, we trade hours of our life for a salary. People say that if you love what you do, you will never work a day in your life. I disagree. Before moving to Hollywood, I worked a few jobs, and all of my employers expected the same from me. I came in when expected, took breaks when expected, stayed when expected, and at the end of two weeks, I was compensated—as expected.

Unfortunately, the amount of compensation was never what *I* expected. Even when I was young I knew if we want more out of life, we must expect more.

We lived in Hollywood for three years, writing and producing for various artists. Besides the gold record, we earned hundreds of thousands of dollars. A couple of twenty-year-old young men with that kind of money in Hollywood, California—can you foresee the problems we ran into? I wish we could have!

While royalties allow you to be paid over and over for the same work, the downside is that if you do not continue to create, the amount of those payments starts to decrease. This happened in our case. As our focus on Hollywood night life increased, our work ethic decreased.

There were friends and family who considered our efforts in the music industry a failure because we did not achieve celebrity status. I feel differently. It is not a failure if you learn the lesson. Hollywood was an opportunity to grow. Hollywood was training ground. Hollywood was a *lot* of experience.

My experience taught me to never get comfortable enough, wherever I was, so I'd lose my fire for whatever got me there.

I also learned to never, ever let anyone's opinion of my dreams become a reality in my mind—especially if they are not living their *own* dream life. Their expectations are just that, theirs.

The chains of the past

After those three years in Hollywood, I returned to Kansas— still not wanting to work for anyone else and still with limited options. For the next few years I worked as an illegal street pharmacist (if you don't mind my using a euphemism).

On December 1, 2004, I had a life-altering experience. I sat in my living room, and for the first time in my life I heard God's voice; there was no way I could misinterpret His words: He told me to *get it together*. Hearing this truly scared me; I like to say it scared me to life, not to death.

That night, I turned everything around.

My girlfriend and I had been living together since I returned from Hollywood, and we had three daughters. Three days later we were solidly married. We started going to church regularly, paying our tithes faithfully, and I served the church with my heart and soul.

After a few months I began to feel stifled, stagnant, and depressed. Although I had made the change to live my life according to God's will, things were still very difficult. It's hard to stay consistent with something you hate doing. I hated working for other people, and nice suits and fresh haircuts do not pay the bills.

I worked a job for a couple of weeks, then I would look at the paycheck I had earned with all my time and effort and never go back. I grew frustrated with myself not being able to provide as I desired.

Fewer than ninety days after my life-altering experience, I learned a very harsh lesson: Bad decisions from the past always have a way of catching up with you.

My wake-up call was being dragged out of my home by police, seeing my wife face down on the kitchen floor in handcuffs and my three daughters at gunpoint as they sat on their beds.

It was a drug raid. The law of reaping and sowing applies to us all. The case was built prior to my salvation, and I was reaping the consequences of my actions. I knew I had let my entire family down.

I sat in the courtroom with my wife and parents in the row behind me and prayed. The Lord answered.

There is man's law and by these laws, I should have spent many years in prison. There is also God's law. I had done a lot of sowing in the community and in our church during the previous ninety days, and while I felt like a failure, God saw my heart. I didn't spend one day in jail. God's law of reaping and sowing prevailed.

I thanked God for my miracle. Safely at home the night of my court appearance, I prayed, "What would you have me to do?"

The next day, I got a call from a local businessman who said he wanted to share something with me over lunch. He introduced me to the idea of network marketing. I had one huge challenge, however—self-doubt. Because of my past, I doubted that people would listen to me or follow me.

In networking, it is important to be able to cast vision and lead, with passion, those with whom you have influence. So, I wrestled with playing full out. I was picking and choosing with whom I'd share my opportunity, avoiding those who I believed were more successful than I was. This was the toughest breakthrough for me.

It took several years, a lot of personal development, and more self-reflection than I had ever done before. Breaking through mental roadblocks created by your past is the toughest, most important, breakthrough to have. It takes a lot of internal evaluation to undress the well-dressed lies you have been telling yourself for years. These are the lies we tell ourselves when we are ready to settle for less than our goal, when we are convincing ourselves the dream is too big, and we begin to negotiate ourselves right off the ledge of our best life.

Fear of the unknown

In 2009, I was introduced to the network marketing company that would change my life. When my wife and I were presented with the opportunity, we did not hesitate. We joined and immediately submerged ourselves into every aspect of personal development. We went to every training event, took notes, listened to every audiotape, and bought every book recommended by the leaders in the industry.

On one Friday evening in 2010, I was up late reading *The Dream Giver*, a book by Bruce Wilkinson. It was a very quick and easy read, an enjoyable story about a visit Mr. Wilkinson made to South Africa, and I was surprised when something happened to me near the end of the book. I was almost finished when I heard the voice of God telling me I should go to South Africa and help free the people financially.

Now, I was thinking the same thing you are probably thinking right now: This is *crazy*!

I had never been to Africa and didn't know a single person anywhere on the continent. I was up the entire night, struggling with the Lord. Around dawn I went to my parents' house for guidance. My vision was so big, I believed they were the only ones who could help me interpret what I was experiencing.

I valued their advice. My father is a bishop and the pastor of our church, and my mother is the co-pastor and a former elementary school principal who was then in the process of starting her own private school.

My wise parents listened to me as I attempted to describe my experience. My eyes were bloodshot from lack of sleep and I was very intense as I told them what I believed God was leading me to do. They advised me to get some rest, pray, and wait for confirmation. After I took a nap, I spent the rest of the day looking at flights to South Africa and trying to make sense of what was happening to me.

On Sunday morning, I woke up for church still in awe of the experience I had the day before. We had a guest speaker, an evangelist from out of state whom I had never met. Toward the end of the sermon, he began to speak to certain individuals, telling them what the Lord was telling him about their situations.

He walked over to me, microphone in hand, and said without preamble or hesitation, "You are called to Africa. I see you in Africa working on some type of business."

I looked over at my father, standing in the pulpit, and he shook his head and took his seat. That was my confirmation.

After the service, my dad told me my aunt worked for the U.S. Embassy and he believed she was stationed in Cape Town, South Africa. It was a sign. When I contacted her and shared my vision, she said only, "When are you coming?"

I had never been to Africa. I felt that four letter word creeping into my spirit. I felt FEAR.

Fear is a very powerful weapon. It is used to control and manipulate people and situations. People use fear to control other people, the enemy uses fear to manipulate our minds. Some fears are rational, and we all have them. Rational fear is our brain's way of keeping us alive. Fear of walking along the ledge of a skyscraper is a rational fear.

However, the worst fears are those internal, irrational fears. People who have an irrational fear of the water will never experience an ocean cruise. People who have an irrational fear of flying may never experience a journey to a different country. Irrational fears keep us from the peak life experiences that make life fulfilling and exciting.

I knew my fear was irrational. Forty-two days later, I boarded the sixteen-hour flight to Cape Town, South Africa.

The moment I touched down in Africa, my fear vanished and I was overcome with excitement and intense purpose. It was a surreal and deeply spiritual moment. I could write an entire book about the forty days I spent in South Africa.

My decision to break through the fear of the unknown, to take that leap of faith, and to follow the dreams that God put in my heart, opened the door for tens of thousands of people to change their lives.

Since then, I have made dozens of trips to eleven different countries, coaching, teaching, training, and empowering people to take their own leap of faith and to follow their dreams.

When God gives you a vision, it is never just for your own benefit. Breaking through those fears was not just for me but for the thousands of people who were waiting to join me on this journey.

My experiences have taught me some very important life lessons.

First, when it comes to business, always look for a way to create residual income. Write a book, score a film, write a song, build a team-building business. A quote by Warren Buffet comes to mind, "If you do not find a way to make money while you sleep, you will work until you die."

I don't want to run a business only to find out it runs me. Even worse, I don't want to sacrifice my dreams by getting hired to build someone else's dreams.

Second, the three ingredients to being successful in life are persistence, perseverance, and posture. You must get after it, stay after it, and do it with confidence.

Lastly, I learned that in everything you do, the key to breaking through is to take immediate action, even when you are gripped by fear. Taking action turns your fears into your fuel.

To God be the glory, and I will see you at the top.

Biography

Arturo Lassiter is a true entrepreneur at heart. As soon as he graduated from high school, he moved to Hollywood, California, where he was a successful singer, songwriter, and vocal producer for Universal Records. He earned a gold album for his songwriting talent.

Lassiter has also proven to be a dynamic leader and trainer in the direct sales industry. From his hometown of Topeka, Kansas, he built an organization of more than ten thousand representatives in twelve countries all over the world by helping others pursue their dreams and goals.

Lassiter earned a bachelor's degree in organizational leadership and transformation change from Friends University. He is a husband, a father, and man of great faith.

Contact Information:

Phone/Text: 785.969.2826
Email: cuatdatopglobal@gmail.com
Social Media: Arturo Lassiter

CHAPTER SEVENTEEN

The Lovely
Overcomer

E.B. Cole

My grandparents were working-class folks with Christian values. They raised seven children in Hanford, California, a farm town halfway between Los Angeles and San Francisco. After high school, my mom attended San José State University, where she met my father, a wild child from West Philadelphia and a Vietnam vet.

Within a year, they were married and expecting my sister Tammy. When I was born four years later in 1980, their marriage was in trouble. My father was drunk and high in the delivery room, and he didn't show up when she and I checked out of the hospital.

When we finally made it home, Dad was loading Mom's belongings onto a U-Haul, and he said, "I don't want to be married to you anymore."

Mom landed a full-time gig at the phone company and found an apartment for the three of us, but she was barely making ends meet as a college dropout and single mother.

Things became too stressful for her to cope, and when I was two, she asked Dad to take care of my sister and me until her finances improved. Dad didn't hesitate; in fact, he took my mother to court and the judge awarded him custody.

Dad worked full-time as an electrical engineer and owned a small three-acre farm in East Palo Alto—our own little utopia and a wonderful place to grow up. All my good childhood memories are from that time. We were safe behind the fence surrounding our little piece of heaven on earth, but the town was riddled with drugs, poverty, and violence.

Why would my father expose us to a place like that? Dad was a drug dealer as well as an electrical engineer, which I didn't learn for years.

Christmas Day, 1989, was the day my life changed irrevocably. My sister and I woke up to no tree, no gifts, and no Dad. We found out he had been arrested on drug charges.

Dad went to prison and my sister and I moved in with Mom. I matured fast physically while emotionally I was still a nine-year-old girl. The neighborhood boys would corner me and feel me up. I didn't realize they were assaulting me, but I hated what they did and it made me feel awful. I began wearing baggy clothes to hide my rapidly developing curves.

Two years went by, and I was a handful. My grades had plummeted and my behavior was atrocious. When Dad got out of jail, my parents decided I should live with him in East Palo Alto while Tammy stayed with Mom.

One day at school, a group of eight or ten boys surrounded and taunted me, then they groped and grabbed my breasts and crotch. I begged the boys to stop, but they didn't, and dozens watched as the boys tormented me. When the principal eventually intervened, I broke free and ran home crying.

My dad found out about it and asked what *I* had done to have them treat me that way as if *I* had provoked the attack. I felt abandoned, ashamed, and violated. A few months later when Dad moved back to Philadelphia without me, I was sure he didn't love me anymore, especially after he called me a little bitch.

I went buck wild. My mom tried to get me into counseling, but I just didn't care. Instead, I joined a gang and started robbing, stealing, selling drugs, drinking, smoking weed, and soon I was having sex.

I ran away for days at a time, and when Mom changed the locks, I'd break into the house. Once I went to San Francisco to sell drugs. I was introduced to an older man who seemed to be harmless-looking, right up to the moment when he raped me. He didn't finish the act because I stabbed him, just not badly enough to kill him.

By this point, I didn't give a damn about anything. When I got caught by the police with dope on me, I tried to play my *I'm sorry, officer, I won't do it again* routine, but it was past curfew. The officer put me in handcuffs and told dispatch to call my mom.

"Take her to juvenile hall," Mom told the dispatcher.

During my 48 hours in juvie, I was tested and discovered I was pregnant. I was just 13 years old and didn't know what to do. When I was released, I hung out on the streets, drinking, smoking weed, and doing my best to avoid the issue. By the time I decided to have an abortion, I was so far into the pregnancy I couldn't bring myself to follow through. I left the abortion clinic screaming and crying out to God, asking Him to help me. As I cried, a feeling came over me that everything was going to be okay. I yelled, *Okay, God, I trust you! Thank you!*

I received confirmation from Him, I heard His voice; I knew I would be all right.

By the time I entered my freshman year at an alternative high school for troubled kids and pregnant teens, I had a baby boy, and I was still a handful—motherhood didn't stop me from being reckless. I was still gang-affiliated, and I'd drop my baby off at daycare and hang out until school let out.

Things started to get better when I was fifteen. Mom bought a house in Stockton, and over the next several years, I calmed down long enough to complete my GED.

When I turned 18, I moved into my first apartment. I worked two jobs to keep a roof over my head, waiting tables and working security at a nursing home.

When I was 21, I met Angel. He was handsome, charming, and had a great sense of humor, but he was a pimp like his father. When we moved in together, it didn't last long. At the time, I was doing meth and sometimes cocaine. We argued, and it wasn't pretty. I came to know his true character when Angel tried to make me work for him, but not soon enough; I was pregnant.

Though I knew Angel would have nothing to do with our baby, I couldn't bring myself to have an abortion. My friends thought I was crazy for even contemplating another child, but it was my decision and my choice. I told my mom about the pregnancy, and she was angry. Despite that, she eventually got over it and was as supportive as she'd been with my first son.

After I landed a great position at a teaching hospital in Sacramento, I discovered the commute from Stockton was just too long, so I searched for a place closer to work. I'd be leaving all my support behind in Stockton, but I was ready to be away from my safety net because the help came with plenty of criticism.

My new landlord introduced me to Alvin, her son and maintenance man, and told me to call him with any problem. He was charming and said all the right things, including that he was legally separated from his wife, so we began to date. Soon he charmed me into a sexual relationship.

When I became pregnant, I knew I wasn't ready for another child and neither was he. Then I learned he had seven kids and no plans for divorce, and I arranged for an abortion.

Alvin took me to the clinic, but within a few days, he was a ghost, cutting all ties and communication. Though I knew to end the relationship was necessary, my conscience was eating away at me, so I made a huge mistake and called Alvin's wife, Saundra, to apologize for my behavior.

Saundra reassured me sweetly, "Oh, baby, it's not your fault. You're young, you didn't know any better."

That evening there was a knock at the door, and Saundra was outside with two teenage children. She politely asked to come in, but the moment she was in the door, she turned vicious, yelling, "It's a good thing you killed that baby because I would have murdered you and that baby both!" While I stood there holding my toddler, she punched my face and her kids shouted obscenities at me.

With tears streaming down my face, I begged them to leave. The police came and took a report, but they didn't take the incident seriously.

Saundra's rage didn't stop. She stalked me at my job, my house, and phoned at all hours. After weeks of terror, I moved back to my mom's house in Stockton where I felt safe. I obtained a restraining order and thought this would surely stop the harassment.

Meanwhile, I was promoted and was moving up the career ladder. I began to date Daniel, a co-worker, and we decided to move in together. Almost nine months had passed and I felt safe moving back to Sacramento.

At the office one day, I got a call that Saundra was at the front desk asking for me. I didn't panic; I had the restraining order and an upcoming court date to extend it. I contacted the campus police and they escorted her off the property.

Several weeks later, Daniel and I were at home, the kids were in bed, and we were talking, but he was a bit high and our discussion turned into an argument. One thing led to another and I threw a large glass of sweet tea at him. Daniel did *not* find it funny, so I decided to sleep with the kids.

Hours later, Daniel woke me up; the police were there. I went to the door and they said, "Put your hands behind your back. You're under arrest." I was arrested for stalking, making terroristic threats, and child endangerment, booked, strip-searched, and put in a holding cell.

With my one call, I called Daniel, but he told me we were through. He had already called my mother to pick up my children and my dad to get my belongings.

I was in jail for several days before I finally met my public defender and he explained the charges. They were totally fabricated, but it was easier for the district attorney to believe a tale of fatal attraction than a husband and wife ganging up on the former mistress.

My bail was set at $2 million, and since I didn't have the $100,000-$200,000 needed to post bail, I stayed in jail until my trial. I had lots of company; it seemed like all the women facing major time were there because of a man.

Faith was the only thing that got me through, and I spent most of my jail time on my bunk reading my bible. I knew God would turn things around for me. I just had to have faith and trust in Him.

Days before the trial, my attorney brought the D.A.'s offer: Plead "no contest" to two misdemeanors of stalking and terrorist threats, agree to a 10-year restraining order, no firearms for 10 years, and community service—and I could be out the next day with time served.

Though I was innocent and this would give me the stigma of being a criminal, I *was* guilty of messing with another woman's husband, so I rationalized the plea was my punishment for committing adultery. The tradeoff was I'd be reunited with my kids, and I could begin to put my life back together again. I took the deal and got out the day after my 26th birthday.

While I was incarcerated, I had reached out to my older sister and her husband in Virginia and they offered to let the kids and me stay with them until I got on my feet. I had $500 to my name and two kids in tow; I prayed to the Lord, asked him for guidance and to put me on the path he chose for me, and He did.

In Hampton Roads, Virginia, I saw positive prospects and an opportunity to reinvent myself. No one knew me or my past. I found a local church and the kids and I began attending.

My first job was waitressing at a truck stop, making $2.60 an hour plus tips. Within nine months I had my own apartment, a beat-up car, two jobs, plus I was completing my community service as part of my sentencing. My volunteer work was as a crisis interventionist, and I received training on handling crisis calls, specifically suicidal callers. The work was very rewarding, and I loved helping and counseling others in a crisis. After my mandated time, I continued as a volunteer and eventually was hired on staff.

And yet, I backslid. I went out with new friends from my multiple jobs, looking for a military man with benefits and living allowances. I attended church less frequently and focused on my pursuit of a suitor to pay my bills. One night I spotted Keith, a Virginia boy from a good home.

I had spent my entire adult life and much of my childhood bouncing from one man to another. Keith was my fairy tale, an opportunity to have a marriage and happily ever after. At first, things were good. I had someone who loved me, who could hold down a job, and I knew my ambition would eventually rub off on him. As our love grew, I continued to climb the corporate ladder. I was moving up so fast I could barely catch my breath. The one area in my life where I always excelled was my career, and I knew someday, somehow, I'd achieve all my dreams.

When I became pregnant, we moved in together and prepared for the birth of our son. Keith was there throughout the pregnancy and was a father figure to my two boys. We discussed marriage, which seemed to be the natural progression in our relationship.

After our son was born, Keith landed a good job that required him to travel most of the time. Our relationship deteriorated, he soon had a girlfriend, and when he finally packed up his belongings and went to his parents' house, I felt embarrassed and worthless. I called my mom, crying; I was sure she would console me, but she said, "Girl, stop crying! Lick your wounds and put your big-girl panties on. Life is not a fairy tale and you're not Cinderella. Move on!"

First I was shocked, then I realized, "She's right, I need to move on, he wasn't all that perfect anyway."

I continued to move up the corporate ladder and was recruited for a job in Northern California with a six-figure salary. After seven years away, I was excited to be back. I was barely 33, and on the surface, I was a success. I had beat the odds, owned my own home, accomplished things that I never dreamed I could—all on my own, with my kids in tow, no life partner in sight.

Underneath the surface, though, I was a very angry, lonely, and tortured soul, and I began to drown my feelings in gallons of my go-to alcoholic beverage. At first, the drinking was social and I was the life of every party, but very soon I was drinking on my own. Because I'd never addressed my core issues—anger, resentment, and abandonment—and alcohol was the only way I knew to numb the emotional pain, my drinking rapidly went out of control.

The slightest thing would set me off, and I began to lash out at anything and everyone. I threw fits, very much like a toddler's tantrum. All my relationships, both personal and professional, suffered.

There was no denying I'd become the very thing I despised most about my father—an addict. Surely this was not a way for me to live. I found myself on my knees, welcoming death, begging God to remove me from life. I was so far gone, I didn't worry about my children and figured they'd be better off without me. God *did* intervene. I sought life instead of death, checking myself into rehab.

Rehab was nothing at all like I expected. It humbled me.

I began to work the 12-step Alcoholics Anonymous program. I accepted I had no control over my drinking, my life was unmanageable, and I came to believe that a higher power would restore me to sanity. . . but *I had to do the work.* As I trusted the process and worked the steps, I had a spiritual awakening. The more I worked the program, the closer to God I became.

I made amends with those who harmed me, forgave them, and most of all, I forgave myself. However, this was only the beginning. To maintain my sobriety, I practice the twelve steps daily. In every situation I find myself powerless, I work the steps. This became my new normal. I no longer lash out or blame others; my job is to practice love and tolerance in every situation. I put away my childish behaviors and reactions to life's unpleasantries and seek guidance from my higher power. At last, I've found peace and serenity. I know absolutely that God created me in His perfect image. Regardless of poor decisions and relationships in my past, I know who I am and I know God created me to do good works. I have wisdom and my purpose is to share my wisdom and find ways to help others.

I've learned that our change only comes when we accept the fact that we need help, when we embrace our vulnerability, begin to set boundaries, restructure our lives, and practice discipline. Once we've decided to grow, there's no turning back. Change is the defining moment in time—a time of coronation, rebirth, and walking into our purpose.

This is only a start. To achieve our true greatness, we must forgive ourselves daily, and forgive the past traumas that we cannot change. Forgiveness doesn't change the past, but it does change the future. Glory be to God!

Biography

The younger of two girls E.B. was born in Northern California to working-class folks who soon divorced. Growing up in the Silicon Valley, she was a latchkey kid. When she became a mother at the age of fourteen, she felt disregarded and abandoned, and never anticipated that somehow she would survive abuse, addiction, and incarceration, much less achieve her dreams. E.B. knows she is nothing short of a miracle; when others counted her out, God counted her in. She was determined to turn her life around and began to contemplate and pursue ways to help others overcome their own adversity.

Despite the odds stacked up against her and her lack of college education, she became a homeowner and an executive in the health-care industry with a six-figure salary.

A mother of four, she lives in Blythewood, South Carolina—a business mogul, entrepreneur, mentor, and now an author. She founded Midlands Legacy of Hope & Healing, a charitable organization with a mission to remove the stigma associated with mental health and substance abuse disorders.

E.B. said, "What do you do when you realize God's grace is sufficient and dreams do come true? You write! My life and my story of trials and tribulations are testaments to God's grace and mercy."

Contact Information

Email: TheLovelyOvercomer@gmail.com
Facebook: The-Lovely-Overcomer
Twitter: @LovelyOvercomer
Instagram: IamLoveleE33

Chapter Eighteen

Escape the Ordinary

Nik Halik

As a child, you used to dream. Your mind wasn't shackled by logic, false beliefs, or societal limitations. Everything was possible, and the world was wondrous and magical. Then, as you aged, you started developing false and limiting beliefs about yourself and the world around you. You started buying into societal programming. When people told you something wasn't possible, you believed them. When your peers chose jobs and careers based on their own internal limitations, you followed suit. You started thinking more "responsibly" and "sensibly." And in this process, the flame of your dreams died down to mere embers, and in some cases may have been entirely extinguished.

My invitation to you is to breathe life into your dreams again. Cast off the shackles of your false beliefs and societal programming. Realize the vast majority of your limitations are only in your mind.

What would you do if money was no longer the primary reason for doing or not doing something? What grand adventures would you live? What noble causes would you champion? What great feats would you accomplish?

I was born with a poor biological template. I developed chronic allergies, debilitating asthma, and I was nearsighted. I was medically confined to my bedroom for the first decade of my life. When I was eight years old, a traveling salesman knocked on our front door in Port Melbourne, Australia, and sold my non-English speaking Greek immigrant parents a set of the Encyclopedia Britannica. That set turned out to be one of the greatest influences on my life. It was the spark and secret kindling that set my imagination on fire. My imagination had stretched my mind, and it would never retract to its original dimensions.

I read the encyclopedia constantly and, without my parents knowing, I'd take it to bed with me. I'd shine a flashlight under the sheets, flick the pages of a volume through to a subject that fascinated me, and read until I nodded off to sleep. Sometimes I'd stay awake past midnight, dreaming about the things I was going to pursue in life, and imagining the world that was out there waiting for me.

Growing up, an inspirational character for me was the comic book adventurer named Tintin. Tintin was living the "never grow up" dream, and I traveled the world through his pages, taking in every exotic detail. I read and reread Tintin books in our school library, daydreaming about his magical life. In his various adventures he was a pilot, space explorer, mountain climber, and deep-sea diver. He also climbed the mountains of Nepal, rescued African slaves, battled pirates, and dived down to the deepest abyss of the ocean to explore shipwrecks.

When I reflect on the adventures of Tintin, I realize my

childhood dreams have come true. Many times, in the course of my adventures, I've been in some far-flung destination and had a weird feeling of déjà vu—a Tintin flashback. I was fascinated by space travel. Growing up, I was glued to the TV watching the United States and Russian launches.

Space travel was the big deal then. All this adventure fueled my desire to get in a rocket ship and go myself.

The encyclopedia, the lure of space travel, and the Tintin adventures opened up all the things I wanted to accomplish. I sat down and wrote my highest aspirations in life.

Writing the Script of My Life

I drafted my own screenplay of goals. I was the actor, the producer, and the director. Here I am as an eight-year-old, with my list of ten life goals. Pretty ambitious. Dreaming and thinking big. That list has fueled my life. Since writing down that list at age eight, I've accomplished almost everything on the list. I have two major goals remaining: rocketing to a space station orbiting 250 miles above the Earth and walking on the moon. Even those goals are within my reach.

My Adventures

I became the first flight-qualified, certified civilian astronaut from Australia, and was a backup astronaut for the TMA 13 NASA/Russian space mission. I remain in mission allocation status for a future space flight to the International Space Station.

For a few years, I lived in Moscow and graduated from the Yuri Gagarin Cosmonaut Training Center in Star City. During the Communist era, Soviet cosmonauts were quietly chosen, groomed, and trained behind a veil of secrecy.

My life has been filled with extreme adventures. I have visited over 152 countries. I have trekked with the Tuareg Bedouins across the Sahara Desert. I broke the sound barrier in a modified Russian MIG 25 supersonic interceptor jet traveling at almost Mach 3.2 (2,170 mph, 3,470 kmh) and viewed the curvature of the earth. My rock band performed and toured with big names like Bon Jovi and Deep Purple. I dived down five miles deep in a pressurized biosphere to have lunch on the bow of the shipwreck RMS Titanic in the North Atlantic Ocean.

I have climbed the highest peaks of five continents, including the mighty Mt. Aconcagua in the Andes. I have two more peaks to summit on my attempt to become one of a handful of climbers in history who have climbed the Seven Summits—the highest mountains of all seven of the world's continents. I did a Navy Seals HALO skydive jump with oxygen, above the summit of Mt. Everest in Nepal at over 30,000 feet, on my most recent birthday. I have rappelled into the heart of the most active volcanoes in the world. I have storm-chased tornadoes in the Midwest and hurricanes across the Atlantic Ocean.

I even negotiated with the former deposed dictator of Egypt to spend a night in the nearly 5,000-year-old Cheops Pyramid in Giza, Egypt. I spent the night alone in the King's Chamber of the pyramid and slept in the sarcophagus in total darkness—the very same sarcophagus that Napoleon Bonaparte, Alexander the Great, Herodotus, Sir Isaac Newton, and other giants of history had slept in. Media outlets dubbed me the "Thrillionaire."

"Don't be an extra in your own movie"
—Bob Proctor

My Worldwide Business

During the last two decades, my companies have impacted more than one million people in fifty-seven countries. I deliver keynote speeches and facilitate entrepreneurial training courses around the world. I even get the opportunity to speak in remote locations most foreigners would simply never visit. Just recently, I spoke in the communist "hermit kingdom" of North Korea and taught geography to a classroom of teenagers about to graduate. I have conducted an entrepreneurial mastermind seminar to more than 750 investors and business owners in Tehran, Iran.

Do not go where the path may lead, go instead where there is no path and leave a trail.
—Ralph Waldo Emerson

It's Time to Live Your Dreams

My adventurous life did not happen because I was born into wealth. Lacking a wealthy friend such as Tintin's Captain Haddock, I realized that if I wanted to become an adventurer like Tintin, I would need to develop multiple pillars of income in order to afford such a lifestyle. I wasn't born rich—but I was born rich in human potential. My life by design was never coincidental or lucky. I have merely acted out the script I created for my life—a screenplay I wrote as a young child. My manifested reality was the result of every decision made in my life. I did have medical issues earlier in my childhood, but I refused to be held captive by them. I was forced to clear any obstacles that threatened to obstruct my path of self-discovery.

I'm no more special than anyone else. I've simply set my sights on big goals and have never stopped working to achieve them. There's nothing stopping you from doing the same. You may not care about traveling or anything else I've done. I don't share my life experiences with you because I think you should care about anything I've accomplished, but rather to simply inspire you to live your own version of the ideal life.

There is no shortage of adventures to live and thrills to be experienced. You may want to live on the beach and surf every day. Perhaps you want to go on an epic RV trip. Your dream could be to do frequent humanitarian trips to developing countries. Maybe you just want to spend more time with your family or simply have the leisure time to read more.

Whatever it is for you, go after it. Don't let anyone tell you it's impossible; don't let anything stop you. Life is the greatest show on earth. Ensure you have front-row seats. You have an abundance of opportunities that people in the past could not even have dreamed of. Eliminate all excuses from your mind and vocabulary. Cut off the pessimists and haters in your life. Surround yourself with inspirational people, and immerse yourself in inspirational material. Do whatever it takes to escape the trap of the ordinary. Because I can promise you this:

It is so worth it.

"Start by doing what's necessary; then do what's possible; and suddenly you are doing the impossible"

—St. Francis of Assisi

Biography

Nik Halik, The Thrillionaire® Entrepreneurial Alchemist, Civilian Astronaut, Extreme Adventurer, Keynote Speaker is the founder and chief executive officer of Financial Freedom Institute, Lifestyle Revolution, and 5 Day Weekend®. He became a multimillionaire and amassed great wealth through investments in property, business, and the financial markets. Nik's group of companies have financially educated and life coached more than 1 million clients in 57 countries. Nik generates passive income, building recurring subscription businesses, investing in tech startups, and multi-family apartment complexes. He is currently an angel investor and strategic adviser for several tech start-ups in the United States.

Halik has traveled to more than 150 countries, dived to the wreck of RMS Titanic to have lunch on the bow, been active as a mountaineer on some of the world's highest peaks, performed a high-altitude low-opening (HALO) skydive above the summit of Mt. Everest in the Himalayas, climbed into the crater of an exploding erupting volcano (1,700 degrees F) for an overnight sleepover, and just recently, entered North Korea to expose a sweatshop factory operating illegally for an American conglomerate.

He was the back-up astronaut for the NASA / Russian Soyuz TMA-13 flight to the International Space Station in 2008. He remains in mission allocation status for a future flight to Earth's only manned outpost in orbit—the International Space Station with Russia.

Contact Information:

www.FollowNik.com

CHAPTER NINETEEN

It's Who You Know*

*and how you handle the relationship

Nate 'Millz' Gray

Networking and relationship building are crucially important to your career at all levels, and they're also essential to your everyday life. In my case, making just one powerful connection helped to catapult my career and my life to a much higher level.

I'm sure you're familiar with the saying, *It's not* what *you know, it's* who *you know*. Have there been times you learned about an important person you were talking to or standing next to—*after* the fact? Do you know the magic of being in the right place at the right time?

It happened to me when I made a valuable contact, a connection that created a monumental shift in my life and career. It happened when I bumped into Dwight Pledger, a friend and protégé of the world-renowned motivational speaker,

Les Brown. Since our accidental meeting, Dwight has become my mentor, and just as importantly, he's my friend.

When the opportunities you've dreamed of and worked toward happening, often they're nothing like you imagined. Keep an open mind and expect surprises.

Identify your ideal connections. Even if your industry seems to be over-saturated, having the right contacts will help you rise above the competition if you are pulling your own weight. First, you need to do some research to determine the key players in the game in your industry or profession. Check local events in your area that are related to the nature of your business to see which people are attending. Determine the people with whom you'd like to meet and make connections.

Social media is also a way of connecting with like professionals in your industry no matter where they're located. The reach and transparency of Twitter, Facebook, and Instagram give you more opportunities to follow other professionals and see their latest events or projects.

Attending conferences, trade shows, and seminars can be worth the investment because you exponentially increase your opportunity to connect with leaders in your industry as well as other like-minded individuals. Often the connection you need is sitting right there in the audience with you.

In my experience, attending seminars and conferences has been beneficial; I've made crucial contacts and gained knowledge of the industry. Sometimes these contacts are what I call *hidden connections*—you only made these specific connections because *you were there*. If you'd skipped attending meetings where the important people were, you'd have never been able to make the connections.

When I was first introduced to public speaking, a big part of my networking and promotional strategy was attending book marketing conferences and seminars. I heard Les Brown's name from every speaker on stage wherever I attended a seminar or a conference in the United States. From the moment I first heard his name, I knew he was someone with whom I needed to connect. Every additional repetition reinforced this belief.

I had reached a critical point in my career when I published my first book, *From Him to Us*. I was still finding my way around the speaking industry and learning quite a bit about key people and all the subtleties this business entailed, and I was exhausted from attending book publishing seminars and networking conferences. Facing uncertain times, I started to doubt myself, wondering what my chances were in this industry if I should continue, or perhaps even pursue another field.

Of course, I never backed off. I kept pushing and took my hits and losses as learning lessons. Once I realized I was ready and willing to find a mentor and accept some additional direction, I decided to continue on this path.

Although I'd decided I would no longer invest in attending conferences, one sunny day I was working on my laptop in my Chicago apartment and felt inspired. I said to myself, "Maybe I still have an event in me," and searched the internet for Les Brown events, knowing the attendees would include the connections I needed to make. An intriguing event in Houston caught my eye, and I knew instantly that I must attend. The meeting was TWEF IFLS (Texas Women's Empowerment Foundation International Financial Leadership Summit), a three-day weekend networking conference created by the self-made businesswoman and community leader, Deavra Daughtry.

Les Brown headlined the event, and it sounded like the perfect networking opportunity for me. At the time, I did not have a clue that this was where I would get the life-changing help I needed. I was prepared to focus for the three days of the conference and signed up for all the events, down to the hotel lobby networking.

I'd been privileged to meet Les Brown the year before when he came to Chicago for a conference. That had to be the absolute luckiest day of my life, and you can follow my YouTube channel to learn what happened. I hoped to meet Les Brown again in Houston.

I had just lost my job due to a corporate reorganization and downsizing, so the decision to attend the conference was a big commitment. I flew out of Chicago with positive energy, my faith, copies of my book, and a prayer for a successful event.

Recognize the magic when it happens. By the end of the first night of the conference, I'd done a lot of networking, sold quite a few copies of my book, and I'd had the opportunity to meet the late Dr. Myles Munroe, which in itself was worth the trip. I thought I was done making connections for the night.

I was in the elevator headed back to my room, and this is when the magic happened for me. Only one other man was in the elevator, and the white letters on his black t-shirt caught my eye: *Live Your Dreams*. There was a strong positive energy and vibe between us as we acknowledged each other at the same time. He introduced himself simply: "I'm Dwight Pledger."

"I'm Nate Gray, author and speaker from Chicago."

We exchanged contact info. Dwight's stop came first, and before he stepped off the elevator he smiled and said, "You know, Les Brown is going to be here."

I grinned back, happy at the words. "Yes, I know! I'd like to see him again. I met him last year when he came to Chicago."

Dwight kept on smiling and said, "Take care," as he got off the elevator.

We were able to build rapport as we continued to meet during the conference, and soon Dwight mentioned that he was a Platinum Speaker on Les Brown's team. When I was riding up the elevator, I had no idea how powerful and important a connection I was making—Dwight was the one link I needed.

When Mr. Brown took the stage for his part of the session and before he began his speech, he told the audience, "Give it up for my man, Dwight Pledger!"

Part of making connections is about being kind, being open, and not discounting anyone. Because I did all three, I made the connection of a lifetime.

Even during the Houston weekend, I began to feel the positive shift in my speaking career. Motivational speaker and coach Ona Brown headlined a session in place of her dad, Les Brown, due to a scheduling conflict, and the big moment happened as Ona opened up the floor to her fellow speakers. When Dwight took the podium, he told the crowd about the connection he and I made over the weekend, and he announced the group that he would be my mentor and he'd work with me on my story. Dwight was true to his word and he has continued to work with me ever since that day.

I also met Johnny Wimbrey that weekend. Although Johnny and I did not have the opportunity to work together then, our relationship resurfaced as I ran back into him through Dwight, and it directly led to the opportunity to share my story in *Break Through*.

Align yourself with your industry. You need to be in tune with what's happening in the field you choose and make sure you have what you need to compete in the industry and sustain your business. Your faith and connections alone are not going to bring success. You have to really believe in yourself with all your heart, soul, and focus, and also put the work into it!

Put yourself in among the people you want to align with. Sometimes that alignment can be an alliance, teaming up with the right people and tapping into resources to boost your goals and career. Sometimes the magic happens when you are not expecting it. Sometimes the things you work for may not always appear in the form you expect them to manifest.

The "magic" doesn't happen because there's some magical wand, it happens from all the hard work and seeds you've planted over time. Eventually, opportunities will start opening up for you in many ways beyond what you could even imagine.

You need to continue to work to strengthen the rapport and maintain your relationships. The mentorship that led to the friendship that I still have with Dwight today was started at that first moment we met in Houston, and I have worked at maintaining that relationship over the years.

Maintain the relationship, and always be a student. You can never learn too much. You also have to be realistic about timelines and your level of readiness.

Before Dwight and I started working together, I was naïve and thought I'd instantly be able to share the stage with him and Les. Little did I know, I had a lot to learn and a long way to go! The first time I spoke to Dwight after I got back to Chicago, I asked, "When can I start working with you and share the stage with you and Les Brown?"

Dwight chuckled. "That's a work in progress, my friend! First, I will work with you. There are some things we'll do to craft your story and your message."

He was all about finetuning the story and honing the message. We had several sessions, back and forth, and I carefully heeded his feedback. He went deep! This was no easy overnight process. I worked at becoming a sponge and soaking up all the knowledge, and I was careful to keep in touch to follow up on my progress. We worked together back and forth over the phone and I studied Dwight and Les' speaker videos.

This one connection led to far more than just speaking. My relationship with Dwight broadened my network and opened my mind to what is possible.

Think about this for a second: I could have been anywhere in the world that night, or even just sitting on my couch in my apartment back in Chicago, but I was there at that conference because I made a decision and an investment to do so. The relationship formed because I *took action* that made it possible.

I had faced two choices. One was not deciding to take the Houston trip and instead of wondering what would've happened "if" I had decided to go and be amidst the unknown. I could have only speculated or later have regrets.

The other side of life is the side that takes action, and to this day there are no regrets that I was on this side. Whether or not things worked in your favor because you took action, at least you know the results. The benefit of knowing the result is being able to assess your actions to determine what did or did not work well. If the result was not favorable for you, learn from your assessment in order to improve and better yourself.

I know exactly what happened at the event because I was there in the middle of the action. I was *in* the action because I *took* action. There is no need to wonder, *What could have happened if I had gone to Houston?*

There would be nobody to blame but myself for not taking action.

Leave doors open, don't burn bridges. The relationship I have built with Johnny Wimbrey is an example of how relationships can be formed and maintained. Sometimes you make a connection but do not form an instant partnership on the spot. Don't fret. Connections can be used later—sometimes even years later. You can maintain the rapport by leaving a lasting impression so that the doors are open for future communication. Don't make the mistake of burning bridges. By leaving an encounter on a positive note, you will be welcome when you are ready to reach out to that contact.

When you encounter one of your connections again, you will find communication flows easier. When you speak to them, refer to where you met and how, and then state whatever your business or purpose is for wanting to link with them now. Most of the time, a connection will recall meeting you, but I believe it shows respect for the other person's time to reintroduce yourself. The point is that now you have their attention. By now they will know you are interested in linking with them in some way and you are also maybe in the arena they are in. (That is what you would expect, right?) Think about it! If you have a big shot on the phone, that is cool, but they are not there to chat casually and have a good time with you—they have friends for that.

When I reached out to Johnny Wimbrey, I told him that I met him in Houston in 2011 at the TWEF event. Because I knew Dwight was a friend of his, I also mentioned that Dwight is my mentor. I basically told Johnny I saw the good work he was doing that Dwight had shared from his Facebook page, and I was hoping to connect with him soon. I asked him to check out my tribute I did to Les Brown because I knew Les was a mentor to Wimbrey. He replied, "Hey Nate. I am on the road right now. I will check it out." He was true to his word and gave me feedback directly on my Facebook post where I shared the tribute. I stayed connected with his social media, and that is how I heard about the *Break Through* opportunity. I followed his social media to learn more about the motivational speaking industry, and I learned from his motivation videos. I know that my relationship with Wimbrey will only grow from here.

Your network is a web of connections, as is your life. Meeting the right people and making the right connections are imperative, for your life and your career. Think about what happens in your life as a result of some connection. You need a connection to access the world through the internet. Most likely a job you landed, a promotion you got, or a sale you made was through a connection. In order to reach the next level, you must make a connection to the resources holding the keys to that level. I found Deavra Daughtry's event listed online.

My propitious meeting with Dwight only happened because I went through Deavra, who held the keys to these connections at her event. I also met with Les Brown again through Dwight's relationship with him, and I met Johnny Wimbrey for the first time. Without the support of Dwight, Les, and Johnny, I could not have dreamed that I'd make a dent in the business of motivational speaking. I am better equipped for my ongoing growth because I learn from these powerful connections.

Your journey through life is like making a road trip. You cannot reach your destination without making the proper connections with the highways, interstates, or even side roads that make up the route. Make the right connections, don't burn any bridges, and never stop building your network if you are looking to grow and expand in your profession.

Biography

Chicago native Nate 'Millz' Gray is an author and aspiring speaker who lives in Atlanta, Georgia. His first book, *From Him to Us*, is about faith and weekly spiritual inspiration and is inspired by the manner in which Miltz overcame his own life trials and tribulations. His follow-up book, *A Winning Perspective*, is about positive energy, overcoming adversity, and pursuing your dreams and goals despite life's challenges. The book also offers reassurance that you do not need to quit your day job in Corporate America before you start your dream.

He has more than 13 years' experience in Corporate America's health insurance industry, and he's furthering his education in IT Business Management at Western Governor's University. He also continues to hone his craft in writing, publishing, and speaking on positive energy, overcoming adversity, and business networking.

Millz creates music and loves basketball, both playing the game and watching it. He's married to his long-time best friend, Niesha, and his two stepdaughters attend college.

Contact Information

Email: NateGrayZone@gmail.com
Website: NateGrayZone.com
Twitter: @nategrayzone
Instagram: @nategrayzone
Youtube: Nate Gray Zone
Facebook: Nate Gray Zone

His books are available for purchase through www.amazon.com
and www.NateGrayZone.com

CHAPTER 20

Everything You
Go Through
Is Necessary

Tiffany Brickhouse

A t the very moment you read this passage, your life is beginning to shift. By taking the time to absorb the words in this book, you are bringing a new perspective to your life. Your inner desire to become stronger prompted you to pick up this book in search of answers.

The ominous time we're living in has us asking ourselves hard questions while we do our best to determine if we're part of the problem or the solution. Faced with political insecurity, social injustice, economic uncertainty, racial tension, and a global health crisis, we are all forced to master our resilience.

Every person with a moral compass—and even some without one—have asked the question at least once, *Why is this happening?* More directly, we ask ourselves, *Why is this happening to me? Why* **me?**

We ask from a place of confusion and distress, and we try to figure out why we get so much bad karma when all we want is to do good.

If you're anything like me, you begin to assess your life to see where you went wrong. You start to wonder about the decisions you've made. You wonder who you've mistreated in times past. You wonder if you've dredged up some wicked payback. You take on blame and guilt for something you may not have even done.

But here's the shift: I'm *glad* you had those thoughts. I'm *glad* you've had those concerns. I'm *glad* you've experienced guilt and shame. Why? Because now you know how to identify them. Now you know where to start working. I'm here to tell you, my friend, that everything you've been through, *everything* you're going through is necessary!

You will find the realities of the existence hint of your calling long before you began to walk in it. When I was at my lowest, I began to remember that I'd been considered a leader when I was young. I'm not sure how you would define a true leader, but most people I encountered had always told me, "You move differently," and "I've always looked up to you."

Many of these positive affirmations came about because I adopted some of the character and grace that my mom bestowed upon me while raising me. I picked up maturity through my reading and writing, and I never really followed the crowd. Even when I tried, I never quite fit the mold.

The thing is, I never paid much attention to those affirmations because I wanted to be accepted. I wanted to be equal. I never wanted to be looked up to; I wanted to be *down,* in the know, one of the girls. I should have known better. I should have realized that being equal is valued by what you equate yourself to. You are the sum of those with whom you make company. You are, by cliché, guilty by association. But, when you are made to stand apart, you will be set apart one way or another.

A greater power knows how to set you in a place where you must stand alone to learn your place and purpose in life. You will likely come to this place as the result of a life-altering experience, and the situation will cause you to question what took you there. It is in this place that you will ask yourself all of the hard questions in a desperate search for answers. You will feel as if you are all alone until you begin to take notice of all the red flags and warning signs. You will reach an aha! moment, or as the mothers of my church would say, "You'll understand it better by and by."

The *aha!* moment happens every time you move from one level of consciousness to another. Please know, it will happen more than once. It's the beauty of growth; it never stops.

It is important to understand that you can't stay in the same place forever. You are destined to grow into something new as your mind matures thanks to the journey you take, and your purpose expands. You start to understand that your steps are ordered, and the outcome is inevitable. However, the direction you take is a choice.

I've learned that crisis breeds creativity.

There are phases that will bring you to your epiphany, those *aha!* moments. The first of them will be your desire. As you move through life, you grow with hopes and dreams. On a grandiose scale, this is called vision, and when you speak of your hopes and dreams, you're *casting vision*. Now, I must warn you to be careful when you cast your vision out into the universe because it has a way of walking you right onto its path. Realize that when you speak your vision, you give it life! (Also be mindful that you can give it death as well.)

My vision is to speak to and for people. The irony of my dream is that I have always been a quiet introvert. I never really said much as a child. All of my thoughts translated into written works. I loved writing songs, and I'd share them with my dearest friends and family, singing until I had no voice left to give. I'd write short literary pieces in the style of C.S. Lewis, Spencer Johnson, and my other favorite writers. My favorite books had allegorical undertones speaking of champions who were meek yet mighty. Never in a million years would I believe that I would be a meek yet mighty champion; but suddenly I aspired to be one.

Desire is always the easy part. There are plenty of things you want in life. The question then becomes what will you do to attain them. Only then do you experience the test of your will.

Self-examination is one of the most common tests of will. When you sit down to map out a plan to achieve your goal, the task becomes daunting. It appears unattainable. You begin to seek out counsel from those closest to you. Here's the drawback to putting your vision in the atmosphere—you very well may encounter that which is assigned to cancel the agenda.

It's imperative that you are careful with whom you share your vision. You know as well as I that someone will tell you and everyone around that you can't achieve such a feat. Surprisingly, it's not because they don't believe you can. They know you can! They predict your failure because of their fear of loss: loss of control, loss of stability, loss of familiarity.

All too often, you become complicit when you empathize with what they lose if you move forward. When your empathy dulls your vision, you take an active role in your own demise. This is a dangerous place to live. When you become too comfortable, you never experience growth.

My demise occurred in a failed relationship from which I felt I had no right to leave. I realized finally that my marriage was the manifestation of what I'd done for most of my life—allowing someone else to dictate the best course for my life. When I finally hit bottom, I walked into a place of separation. Yes, you read that clearly, *I walked* into it.

During my descent, I had stopped doing many of the things I loved to do. I could no longer articulate my thoughts verbally or in writing. I no longer had a desire to sing or associate with friends. I imprisoned myself in a miserable, depressed state. But even in the midst of all of the inner turmoil, I never stopped answering my phone to encourage and guide someone else out of a similar situation. Can you believe that? From a place of inner adversity, the desire to speak to and for others still found its way through.

When you finally reach the point where you are completely broken down, you begin to pay attention. That's when your vision reveals itself to you, and you realize you can only go up from there. It is then that you've reached your push to a purpose. You can, and you will get to the point where you say, "Enough is enough." You will get tired of the same mundane routine of life. The quote from Einstein that says, "The definition of insanity is doing the same thing over and over again but expecting different results," becomes all too appropriate.

From the time I was 13, I was acting from a place of insanity. I was working to please others rather than becoming the person

I was meant to become. That inner being that adopts others' opinions of you will cause you to combat your feelings with the notion that no one understands. Your distorted perception is that others will mistake your cry for help as a cry for attention. That misunderstanding leads you to bottle your cries away. One day, that bottle will shatter, and every small cry will have developed into an explosion of rage and pain.

We've all been through something traumatic. My experiences of underaged drinking, promiscuity, rape, and self-loathing in my youth, then divorce, homelessness, and unemployment in my adulthood, caused me to finally realize someone needs to hear me say *I am broken*. Even more important, I needed to admit to *myself* that I was broken.

We so desperately long for someone to understand what we're going through. There are people who become part of your life who will hear your brokenness and identify with it. In the divine order of things, some people will only accept the truth when they hear it from you. It's like the saying, Game Recognizes Game: You can't speak to something you've never been through. This is where your experiences become necessary! The *aha!* moment has arrived.

You must decide to take your life back. For me, I began to read more and take notes from mentors I never dreamed I'd have the opportunity to meet. My issue was that I didn't see myself reflected among those mentors; they weren't other young women, broken and battered internally, giving life to others who decided to flip the switch.

That was my turning point. I looked up to so many people . . . and none of them looked like me. Those who did were unsung and underappreciated. They were big in small circles. No one had broken my mold just yet. I hadn't connected with the ones that I was assigned to because I hadn't walked into a place deserving of their attention. This is not to say that these figures don't exist. You will learn that everyone cannot receive from everybody—different times call for different voices. Those you are destined to reach will know your voice and identify with you immediately.

You have to go back to the self-examination process. For a contemplative period of your life, you will have to walk into a place of separation from a different perspective. It is a place of selfishness. Yes, selfishness. For so long, I used to predicate my actions and decisions on entities outside of me. When I did so and failed, it gave that little voice another reason to emphasize failure and disappointment.

For instance, I used to always say *I'm doing this for my kids. I want them to see that Mommy can do it!* But I set myself to live up to an unrealistic expectation. The truth was, no matter what I did, I was going to be an example to my children. My error was not focusing on the common denominator of achievement, *me*. Whether I win or lose, it was on *me*. Whether I tried and failed or tried and succeeded, it was *me*. You must come to a point in life to realize that no one can benefit or learn from you if there is no *you*.

So, one day, I realized what my next step would be. I understood why I had gone through it all. I took on the belief that I needed to be the voice of the one who was broken. I knew I had nothing specific to offer. I had no real expertise in any field that I could see in myself. I wasn't a professional. I hadn't mastered the art of the deal. I was not a guru in sales and marketing. But I knew I was a champion of the heart. I knew I was just like those faithful characters I had read about in my youth. I knew that I could connect with people in such a way that they would sense the drop in energy if I weren't around.

I wanted to accomplish something that would be of value to others. I earned my real estate license because I didn't want anyone to be taken advantage of the way my mom had been when she lost her house. From there, I went on to earn my title license because others saw my potential to do more and genuinely connect with people. Next, I obtained my notary certification.

You'll be surprised at what else I committed to—working for a grocery delivery company in partnership with a popular grocery chain.

I took great pride in working in the store. I walked into the store every day, and I used the opportunity to learn everyone's name. I gave everyone I encountered an existence. Why? Because I'd never felt like *I* had an existence. Every day, I'd walk in the door with a smile on my face and greet everyone: *Hi, Dan! Hi, Sue! Hi, Tony!* I commanded the atmosphere in the way I'd lacked for so many years. I took charge of my own existence and created my reality, so much so, that the environment would reciprocate and lift me up when I wasn't feeling my best. It's now reached the point where I don't have the opportunity to speak sometimes because my colleagues beat me to it.

You must command your atmosphere. You have to create, develop, and maintain the space you desire.

Yes, as you read this message, I still work for that delivery company, though I have other commitments and dreams as well. I tell you this because I want you to see what a leap of faith looks like. When the opportunity was presented for me to tell my truth, I took it! I walked out by faith, my friends. I wanted to let the world know that I appreciate every valley I walked through to get to this place of self-love.

It is a daily task to command your atmosphere. You never know how high you can go if you haven't fallen to the low place. You must learn to appreciate your valleys. The freedom begins when you realize that there can't be a valley without a matching peak.

This was my great chance to write and give life to all that I've learned. I wanted to let the world know I am grateful for my journey. It was absolutely necessary for me to speak to you from this place so that you know that a big impact can be made with a small voice.

There is an amazing thing about the valleys in our lives. Though they may seem dark, lonely, scary, and desolate, the sound carries, the vibrations are louder, and the echo is greater. My walk through the valley was necessary to show me the darkest of places and teach me that I carry a light within that will drown out the shadows of fear. The beauty of the valley is the peak that partners it. I encourage you, take every experience as an opportunity to learn. Everything you've been through, everything you're going through, it's necessary!

Rather than looking at how hard the journey may be, look around you to find the resources to help you climb. You know you must climb that peak because from there you can see your horizon.

Develop your voice in a low place so that you can be heard in high places. Someone needs to hear from you. You, my friend, are necessary.

Biography

Tiffany Brickhouse is the founder of Mozellyn, LLC, a family of companies specializing in real estate and financial literacy. With a background in banking and finance, she's an aspiring investor and a literacy teacher who wants to help her clients strengthen their financial ability for homeownership. She's also a licensed Realtor with Weichert, Realtors.

Of all Tiffany's career accomplishments, her proudest has been motherhood and mentorship. Affectionately known as "Momma Brickhouse," Tiffany spends much time counseling and mentoring young people. A former youth leader for Pleasant Grove Baptist Church in Newark, New Jersey, she continues to love and care for all who cross her path.

As a woman who went unheard when she suffered in her youth, she has always wanted to be the ear to hear from anyone who needed to cry out. *Break Through* will be the doorway to reaching those who need to be heard.

Tiffany lives in Roselle, New Jersey, with her mother and her three amazing children, Stacey, Joseph Jr, and Joel.

Contact Information:

Email: mozellyn@gmail.com
Facebook: www.facebook.com/tiffanylmb/
Instagram: www.instagram.com/ladylynb/
LinkedIn: www.facebook.com/tiffanylmb/

CHAPTER TWENTY-ONE

Give Back and Inspire!

Kimber Acosta

I held your hand and told you I loved you. You looked deeply into my eyes. Then your eyes closed for what seemed like an eternity (but was only a moment). You swallowed and nodded your head.

Then you opened your eyes and took your last breath.

At that moment, it all came back to me: my biggest fear as a child was that I would lose you. Today, that fear became reality.

For nearly thirty days and nights, I kept vigil by your side. I watched your monitors, asked hospital staff questions, and listened to beeps and compression sounds from the machines attached to your fragile body. Through every crisis, you fought for your life on the inside—and I fought for your life on the outside, questioning every action the hospital staff took.

My mother had been my world since forever. I looked up to her, respected her, loved her, and cherished her. Whenever she went out, I cried for her and anxiously awaited the hugs and kisses I would receive when she returned. She was my world. All I ever wanted to do was make her proud of me. All I ever wanted was to be just like her.

Then one day my whole world came crashing down. I was 10 years old. I did not quite understand what was happening or why. All I knew was I felt as if my life was ending and I could not breathe.

My mother left me.

I remember vividly her telling me to keep her stuffed Pink Panther and to take care of him until she returned for me. She promised she would come back for me someday and I could give him back to her then. I cried and held on tight to Pink Panther. I slept every night with him. I took care of him. I protected him. All so my mother would be proud of me the day she came back. Days turned into weeks, weeks turned into months, and months turned into years. It seemed as if she was right there in front of me, just an arm's length away, living her life, but I could not reach her or be a part of her world.

Did you ever look at the horizon as a child and think, "If I just keep walking, one day I will be able to touch the sky?" That is how I felt knowing Mother lived so close, yet so far. I would see her. I would run up and hug her. I would beg her to let me come home.

The year was 1984, I was 12 years old. I was losing all hope. The pain inside me was growing beyond my ability to handle it. I wanted to die but at the same time, I wanted to live.

Two years had passed since my mother left and it was just over a year since my dad had been given a choice—his children or his new family over his children. I wanted so much to be back home with mother. I would see her. I would beg her to just let me come home. There was no room in her new life for me. I cried almost every night.

Every day I dragged myself out of bed and forced myself to go on with the day and do my school work. There was no foster system to be trapped in. My second oldest sister and I were two of the few who fell through the cracks. If not for a few families who took us in, I am not sure where we would have ended up.

I was a little girl who had to grow up fast and figure out how to survive and pay her own way in a world about which she knew nothing. I picked rocks out of fields for a local farmer. I detasseled corn, delivered newspapers, cleaned dog kennels, bussed tables at a restaurant, worked in a plastic factory, and whatever else I could throughout those years to make money to survive.

My own determination—my own will to survive—kept me in school. Just when I wanted to give up and lost all hope, in 1984 I was given something to help me hold on. That was the year that the *The Cosby Show* first aired and the show changed my life. It kept me alive. I am not sure if I would be here today if it was not for that show—especially Phylicia Rashad, who played Clair Huxtable, the mom on the show. It was through her character's love for her children that I found a way to survive some of the toughest years of my life.

When I was facing a tough week, I would just tell myself, "It will be okay if I can just hold out until Thursday and see Clair." To see Clair hug her children, give them advice, show them love, and discipline them when they did wrong was touching. When she did those things for them, it was like she was doing that for me. I would sit back and pretend I was one of the Huxtable children and Clair was my mother. I took in her advice, hugs, lectures, and love. Whenever I was at my lowest, thoughts of her being the mother she was on that show saved me.

I remember crying—with a blade in my hand, just wanting the pain of my life to stop. I wanted to erase the years of loneliness and would start thinking that a swipe of that blade would take it all away. But then Clair would pop into my head and I somehow could feel her hugs and heard her saying, "Everything is going to be all right, just have faith."

I would tell myself I just need to hold out until Thursday night when *The Cosby Show* was broadcasted and everything would be all right. I would then put the blade down, take some deep breaths, close my eyes, and pray I could make it another day. Feeling love from a fictitious TV character helped me find my way.

And look, I am here today.

Throughout those tough years, Clair saved my life many times. With pills, blade, or gun in my hands, it was Clair's love for her children that made me put them down. Clair showed me the person and mother I wanted to be. Now all these years later and having raised two amazing sons, I look back and thank God for bringing Clair into my life.

When I was in high school I wrote a letter to Rashad and shared with her some details of my life and told her how her character on *The Cosby Show* saved me. I thanked her for coming into my life and helping me keep my faith at a time when I felt all was lost. About a year later, I received in the mail, a picture of Rashad. On it was written, "Thank you for your nice letter, all the best, Phylicia Rashad."

Her response—her taking the time to respond to my letter—meant a lot to me. To this day, that picture hangs on a wall in my home. Each day before I leave home, I look at Phylicia, smile, and give thanks to Clair, my TV mom, for shining the light down my dark and lonely path I was on.

As my children were growing up, reruns of *The Cosby Show* were on TV. It warmed my heart that I was able to sit and watch the show with them. I told them that if it had not been for Clair, none of us would have been there and how she helped me hold onto my faith at a time when I had none.

Now, I am sure you are wondering where is the Pink Panther? Well, he is right here on my desk above my computer. Taking a break from typing, I looked up into his eyes. He has been with me through the ups and downs, the laughter and tears, the joys and sorrows, and the faith and fear.

So many people gave up on me and said I would never amount to anything. For the life I lived, they said I should have ended up either dead, in jail, an alcoholic, or drug addict.

Despite their lack of faith and because of Clair, I persevered. I got out of that town. Through the grace of God, my list of accolades is long and continues to grow. I took my struggles and used each one to champion others.

My career chose me. It was not what I was studying in college. As a child, I dreamed of being a country singer or an officer for Interpol, but God had other plans for me. Through His guidance, I became a journalist and photographer. My career has evolved into hosting my own show online since 2008 and anchoring a news show since 2009. From there, my career has continued to evolve into producing and directing shows for online and cable.

My career has taken me to all corners of the United States to cover and share stories on youth, elders, business people, tribes, artists, and our environment.

Who would have ever thought some little 10-year-old girl whose mother and father abandoned her would:

- Host the Native American Music Awards red-carpet event live online in front of millions of viewers around the world.
- Be the only photographer physically on the red carpet at the Grammy Awards.

- Follow and photograph Tiger Woods and Notah Begay III all weekend during The Presidents Cup.
- Be on the track of the Indy 500 taking photographs.
- Take a private personal tour with Loretta Lynn before the opening of her museum.
- Be one of two photographers in the pit of Tina Turner's opening night of her 24/7 world tour.
- Be one of only a handful of media to cover "Building Bridges: Religious Leaders in Conversation with the Dalai Lama."
- Have her photographs and writing featured and published online, and in magazines, newspapers, books, tour booklets, newsletters, brochures, music videos, and albums all around the world.
- Have pieces of her work hung in museums across the country and issued as limited-edition prints.

Who would have thought that the same little girl who never finished college would one day get to be the commencement speaker for graduates at a college, sharing her story of triumph?

Me neither, but look at me now.

I have never resented my parents for the choices they made because I would not be who I am today if I did not go through every struggle I faced and learned every lesson life offered. I would not have been able to meet the people I have met or share their stories for others to witness their strengths. All I ever wanted was to make my mother and father proud.

One day in 2015, my phone rang and my oldest sister broke the news that she had stage four triple-negative metastatic breast cancer. Six months later, my mother had a massive stroke leaving her paralyzed on her left side.

Within a year, I sent my youngest son off to the military,

and watched my sister wither away and my mother give up. Through that period, with the help of my oldest son, I put my career on hold and spent many hours weekly on the road to be with my sister and mother.

Every week I would give my mother a hug and as I turned to leave she would cry and beg me to take her with me.

The tables had turned.

Instead of a little 10-year-old girl crying for her mother to take her home, the mother was crying and begging to be brought home. I would have given anything to bring her home. The pain of leaving each week tore me apart.

I wondered if what I felt was the pain she experienced every time I cried for her all those years ago. I never knew the reasons behind what she did or the choices she made. She took the answers with her when she died.

But I had a tough choice myself. My sister never told our mother she was dying and she swore me to secrecy. She did not want to worry our mother; she wanted our mother to focus on getting better.

I had to choose: Do I take our mother to my home more than four hours away or keep her down by the family so that I could also be there for my sister during her last days? Mother did not understand, but how could she? She had no idea her oldest child was dying.

My sister died October 27, 2016. Five months later, on March 19, 2017, my mother took her last breath as I held her hand.

You never realize how close death is until you see someone you love take their last breath.

If a 10-year-old girl can grow up and turn her struggles into triumphs and make a difference for others, so can you. Being homeless was never my biggest fear. My biggest fear was losing my mother. I faced that fear twice. I survived her leaving when I was a child and look at all I have done since. I survived her death as well, though it was just as painful as when she left me behind as a little girl.

I will continue to turn my pains into strength to give back, to rise, inspire, and be my brother's keeper, as we all should be.

Biography

As a producer, director, news anchor, entertainment host, editor, marketing/advertising director, journalist, photographer, solutions authority, and online guru, Kimber Acosta has been setting trends while expanding her career titles and gaining accolades for three decades.

Her career path was set at age 19 after getting stuck in a snowstorm more than four hours from her hometown. After she ran out of money to survive the winter in an unfamiliar town where she lived out of her car and slept on the couches of new friends, she stumbled upon a job opening in the mailroom of a national newspaper with worldwide distribution.

Acosta was hired despite not knowing anything about computers or writing. Whenever she wanted to do something to advance her career, her editor told her "to figure it out." Kimber took that as a sign to follow through with whatever she thought was necessary to succeed.

Through her own determination and compassion for others she has built a self-taught career on lifting others up by continuing to shine a light on those that she felt had been left in the dark.

Kimber brings a multicultural approach to her unique worldview; her ethnic background is a mixture of Turtle Mountain Ojibwe, Canadian Cree, French, and German. She lives in northwest Wisconsin and has two children, Animikii and Miskwagiizhig, whose names mean Thunderbird and Red Sky in Ojibwe.

Contact Information:

Email:
giizhig@gmail.com

Websites:
https://www.KimberAcosta.net
https://www.SynergyAllianceSociety.com
https://Kimber12.WorldVentures.biz

Social Media:
https://www.facebook.com/KimberlieAcosta
https://www.linkedin.com/in/kimberacosta
https://www.instagram.com/dare.to.live.freedom.fighter
https://twitter.com/Kimber_Acosta
https://www.youtube.com/giizhig

CHAPTER TWENTY-TWO

The "Real" You

Les Brown

Sometimes it's not about changing to become the person you *want* to be; it's about changing to become the person you *need* to be. There is a whole big, expectant world out there waiting on you to do the things you were destined to do – and the only obstacle in the way is YOU. Personal growth can help you conquer that obstacle, but you must first be a willing participant.

Once you have decided that you are that willing participant, follow these four easy stages of increased awareness to help you begin this journey to a "new you." Let's take a quick look at how 1) self-knowledge, 2) self-approval, 3) self-commitment and 4) self-fulfillment intertwine to help you consciously step into greatness.

First of all, in order to see yourself beyond your current circumstances, you must master **self-knowledge**. Simply ask yourself, "What drives me?" And then pause long enough to hear your response. Try to understand what outside forces – positive or negative – are influencing your answer. Many of us suffer from what I call "unconscious incompetence." That means we don't know that we don't know, which leaves the door wide open for others to tell us what we think we need to know. Therefore, before you can fully wake up and change your life, you must understand the frame of reference from which you view the world. Study yourself, study the forces behind your personal history, and study the people in your life. This will help liberate you to grow beyond your imagination.

The second, and perhaps most crucial, stage of personal growth is **self-approval**. Once you begin to know and understand yourself more completely, then you must accept and love yourself. Self-hatred, self-loathing, guilt and long-standing anger only work to block your growth. Don't direct your energy toward this type of self-destruction. Instead, practice self-love and forgiveness and watch how they carry over into your relationships, your work and the world around you, opening up the possibility for others to love you, too. If you need help in boosting your self-approval, try these steps: 1) focus on your gifts, 2) write down at least five things you like about yourself, 3) think about the people who make you feel special, and 4) recall your moments of triumph.

When you are committed to taking life on, life opens up for you. Only then do you become aware of things that you were not aware of before. That is the essence of **self-commitment**. It's like the expanded consciousness that comes whenever I commit to a diet. Suddenly, everywhere I turn, there is FOOD! Or how about when you buy a new car? Suddenly you notice cars exactly like yours, everywhere you go. Well, likewise, when you make a commitment – when your life awareness is expanded – opportunities previously unseen begin to appear, bringing you to a higher level. In this posture, you are running your life, rather than running *from* life.

The fourth stage of self awareness is **self-fulfillment**. Once you have committed to something and achieved it, you then experience a sense of success and empowerment, otherwise known as fulfillment. Your drive for self-fulfillment should be an unending quest; a continual sequence of testing self-knowledge, fortifying self-approval, renewing self-commitment and striving for new levels of self-fulfillment. Once you have accomplished a goal and reached a level of self-fulfillment, it is then time to go back to the first stage in the cycle.

These four stages create synergy for a conscious awareness of your personal growth. But what about learning to deal with all this from a subconscious standpoint? A very interesting book I have read entitled, "A Whole New Mind," by Daniel H. Pink, explains that the key to success today is in the hands of the individual with a whole different kind of thinking than what our informational age has molded us to. The metaphorically "left brain" capacities that fueled that Information Era, are no longer sufficient. Instead, ""right brain" traits of inventiveness, empathy, joyfulness and meaning – increasingly will determine who flourishes and who flounders." (Pink, 2007)

I highly recommend that, in the midst of your busy schedule, if you haven't done so already, pick up this book and engage yourself to a fresh look at what it takes to excel. As I mentioned before, the only real obstacle in your path to personal growth and a fulfilling life is you. If everything around you is changing and growing – then change and grow. Do it today. Remember, we are all counting on you to step into your greatness!

Now even after making all of these changes what would you say if someone walked up to you and asked, "Who are you?" Would you stutter or hesitate before giving some sort of answer? Would you make up something that sounded impressive, but that you know isn't exactly true? Well, to accurately answer the question of who you are, you must first get in touch with the person who lives and breathes on the inside of you.

When you know and understand who you were made to be, you can begin to tap into the innate power of your own uniqueness. That power allows you the freedom to no longer let life hold you back because of nonsense based on what you've done or not done. It gives you the positive energy to move forward in spite of those things.

You are a unique individual. Think about it, out of 400,000,000 sperm, one was spared to allow you to be here today. Then once you got here, you came with total exclusivity! I know for a fact, as a twin myself, how you can look like someone else, even sound like that person, yet when you consider the total you, there is only one. Wow! Just let that thought sink down in you for a moment.

Now, hopefully that helps you to realize that there is a certain quality on the inside of you that was given to you – and only you – in order to make a difference in this world. Whatever that quality is, it was not intended for you to sit on it, or waste it away. Oh no, it was given to you for a purpose! You cannot, however, learn what that purpose is unless you look inside and see what makes your existence so special.

Don't waste time trying to find "you" in other people. When you compare yourself to others, or try to be like them, you deny yourself – and the universe – the opportunity to be blessed by the gifts and talents that were given only to you. You are destined to achieve great things in *your* own special way; not in the same manner as your friends, relatives, co-workers, colleagues or even mentors. Doing so will only leave you unsatisfied. When you are not satisfied, regret creeps in.

If you don't know this already, let me share a little secret with you: In order to live a good life – a life full of purpose and resolve – you must live it with NO REGRETS!

Most people go through their whole life with a long "would've, could've, should've" list. The truth of the matter is, once you've lived through a day, an hour, or a minute, it's done. You cannot go back. So get over it! Go forward! There's so much more for you to accomplish that you don't have time to live in the past trying to fix things.

Keep in mind, though, that living in the past and reflecting on the past are two totally different things. You *can* look back –

and you should – in order to determine what it was about certain experiences that brought you joy and satisfaction, or grief and despair; what caused you to grow and expand your horizons, or left you stagnant and short-sighted.

Although you cannot relive the past, you can learn much about yourself as a result of having lived it. That requires a lot of honesty with yourself, as well as a willingness to do **whatever it takes** to reach your destiny. Of all the things you can acquire in this life, the most valuable has to be the knowledge of what role you are to play on this earth, for the sake of your destiny.

My favorite book says to *"Lean not on your own understanding, but in all your ways, acknowledge Him and He will direct your paths."* In other words, don't rely solely on your own insight regarding what your role is. There's a Creator who made you and knows you better than you know yourself. Therefore, in everything you do, in every direction you take, recognize and consult with that Creator. That's what it means to look on the inside – not at others.

Now, you will have a real answer when someone asks, "Who are you?" You can assure them that, without a shadow of a doubt, you are not here by accident. You can articulate with unwavering conviction what it is you were put on this earth to do. **Learn to do this and watch the real "you" shine through!**

Biography

Les Brown is a top Motivational Speaker, Speech Coach, and Best-Selling Author, loving father and grandfather, whose passion is empowering youth and helping them have a larger vision for their lives.

Les Brown's straight-from-the-heart, high-energy, passionate message motivates and engages all audiences to step into their greatness, providing them with the motivation to take the next step toward living their dream. Les Brown's charisma, warmth and sense of humor have impacted many lives.

Les Brown's life itself is a true testament to the power of positive thinking and the infinite human potential. Leslie C. Brown was born on February 17, 1945, in an abandoned building on a floor in Liberty City, a low-income section of Miami, Florida, and adopted at six weeks of age by Mrs. Mamie Brown, a 38 year old single woman, cafeteria cook and domestic worker, who had very little education or financial means, but a very big heart and the desire to care for Les Brown and his twin brother, Wesley Brown. Les Brown calls himself "Mrs. Mamie Brown's Baby Boy" and claims "All that I am and all that I ever hoped to be, I owe to my mother".

Les Brown's determination and persistence searching for ways to help Mamie Brown overcome poverty and his philosophy "do whatever it takes to achieve success" led him to become a distinguished authority on harnessing human potential and success. Les Brown's passion to learn and his hunger to realize greatness in himself and others helped him to achieve greatness in spite of not having formal education or training beyond high school.

"My mission is to get a message out that will help people become uncomfortable with their mediocrity. A lot of people are content with their discontent. I want to be the catalyst that enables them to see themselves having more and achieving more."

Les moved to Detroit and rented an office with an attorney, where he slept on the floor and welcomed his reality stating that he did not even want a blanket or pallet on the cold, hard floor to keep him motivated to strive. In 1986, Les entered the public speaking arena on a full-time basis and formed his own company, Les Brown Enterprises, Inc..

Les Brown rose from a hip-talking morning DJ to broadcast manager; from community activist to community leader; from political commentator to three-term State legislator in Ohio; and from a banquet and nightclub emcee to premier Keynote Speaker for audiences as big as 80,000 people, including Fortune 500 companies and organizations all over the world.

As a caring and dedicated Speech Coach, Les Brown has coached and trained numerous successful young speakers all over the nation.

Les Brown is also the author of the highly acclaimed and successful books, "Live Your Dreams" and "It's Not Over Until You Win", and former host of The Les Brown Show, a nationally syndicated daily television talk show which focused on solutions and not on problems.

Contact Information:

www.lesbrown.com

 thelesbrown

 @LesBrown77

 @thelesbrown

 LesBrown

 LinkedIn@

www.ingramcontent.com/pod-product-compliance
Lightning Source LLC
Chambersburg PA
CBHW060304100426
42742CB00011B/1859